The Leaven of Laughter

for

Advent and Christmas

by

James E. Atwood

Illustrations by Pat McGeachy

Note for Librarians: A cataloguing record for this book is available from Library and Archives
Canada at www.collectionscanada.ca/amicus/index-e.html
ISBN 1-4251-0004-x

Illustrations by Pat McGeachy

Trafford's print shop runs on "green energy" from solar, wind and other environmentally-friendly power sources.

Offices in Canada, USA, Ireland and UK

Book sales for North America and international:
Trafford Publishing, 6E–2333 Government St.,
Victoria, BC V8T 4P4 CANADA
phone 250 383 6864 (toll-free 1 888 232 4444)
fax 250 383 6804; email to orders@trafford.com
Book sales in Europe:
Trafford Publishing (UK) Limited, 9 Park End Street, 2nd Floor
Oxford, UK OX1 1HH UNITED KINGDOM
phone +44 (0)1865 722 113 (local rate 0845 230 9601)
facsimile +44 (0)1865 722 868; info.uk@trafford.com
Order online at:
trafford.com/06-1761

10 9 8 7 6 5 4 3 2

INTRODUCTION

The Leaven of Laughter for Advent and Christmas contains hundreds of stimulating humorous quotes and provocative anecdotes which the busy church professional or volunteer can quickly find and use as leaven for one's sermons, classroom presentations, newsletters, or devotional reading.

The material is organized around 45 themes which are used extensively, though not exclusively, during the Advent and Christmas seasons. The reader will find this resource material useful throughout the year.

Everyone should be intrigued not only by the sheer delight of laughter, but by its versatility. All of us have seen people who were being "talked to death" come back to life with a laugh. We have observed hostile people disarmed by a funny story. We have watched total strangers bond through laughter. We have witnessed people tear down economic and social barriers and begin to trust one another because they laughed together. We have marveled as laughter exposed new and vital truth to a skeptic. We have been glad to see the Gospel take root in people's lives through a joyous laugh. Someone said, "When people are laughing, they are listening and one can talk about anything."

It gives me joy to share *The Leaven of Laughter for Advent and Christmas* with all those who will, in turn, share its treasures with others as they tell God's Good News with a twinkle in their eye.

ACKNOWLEDGEMENTS

I've been asked many times, "Where do you get all these stories and good quotes?" I must answer, It's really quite simple: I've read, looked, listened, laughed and wrote them down. I've also enjoyed a wide and stimulating variety of experience. I was a son and a pupil, later I became a student, an athlete, a Presbyterian pastor to three congregations, a missionary and student worker in Japan, and an activist for peace and justice. I am also a grateful husband, proud father, doting grandfather, the husband of another preacher, and a sport's and travel addict. All of these roles and experiences provide rich grist for the humor mill.

Not only in this volume but in those which are to come, literally thousands of people are responsible for *The Leaven of Laughter*. I'm indebted to the famous and the infamous, to celebrated authors and writers of graffiti. I'm grateful not only to wise men and women, but to simple folk who have lifted my spirits with a bumper sticker. Thanks to the legions of story tellers from the dawn of recorded history and to those who surf the net today sharing laughter, wisdom, and truth. And yes, I'm grateful for the God who laughs at us and puts laughter in our mouths. (Psalms 2 and 126:2)

I'm especially grateful for my father, Harry David Atwood, who was the fountain of laughter in my childhood home. As a boy I was so proud of his repertoire of funny stories that I too experienced his joy as he shared them with others. Dad demonstrated throughout his life that "A merry heart does good like a medicine." (Proverbs 17:22)

I particularly appreciate the work of Dr. Martin Marty, Editor of the journal, "Context" and the editors of "The Presbyterian Outlook". Special thanks to Ross Phares, and David MacLellan, and the late William Sloane Coffin, whose wit and wisdom I have borrowed extensively. The reader will find many anonymous quotes for which I make no apology.

Profound thanks to a new and great friend, Marody (Dee Dee) Faulkner, whose professionalism and editorial expertise rescued me from the tyranny of a summer deadline, which I feared would postpone the publication of this volume.

Lastly, I am very grateful for the stimulating drawings of my friend, fellow retired Presbyterian minister, collaborator, and illustrator extraordinaire, the Rev. Pat McGeachy, of Nolensville, Tennessee, who is also the author of 30 books.

~

CONTENTS

FOR MY DAD,
HARRY DAVID ATWOOD

ANXIETY (TENSION)

"DOC, I'D LIKE TO SEE THINGS A LITTLE LESS CLEARLY!"

A 92 year old man was asked his secret for longevity. He replied, "Well, I got a good start on most people by being born before they discovered cholesterol. I had a lot less to worry about."

~

I got my ulcers and my numerous ills
From mountain climbing on mole hills.

~

The most disturbing thing for the digestive process is to continually think of the digestive process." -

Soren Kierkegaard

~

An anxious man made an appointment with a noted London physician. The Doctor's diagnosis was he needed to relax and laugh. He told him to go and see Grimaldi, the famous clown. "All of London is holding its sides laughing at him," he said. The patient straightened himself and replied, "Doctor, I am Grimaldi".

~

The natural role of 20th century man is anxiety. –Norman Mailer, Playwright

~

A state trooper with his lights flashing pulled a driver over to the side of the road and asked why he was driving without tail lights. The man almost fainted. The officer stated, "It's not that big a deal, sir. Please don't be so upset." The driver replied, "That's easy for you to say, officer. I was towing my Ferrari."

~

1

When you don't know what to do, walk fast and look worried.
—Poster, at The Ford Motor Co.

~

If you want something done correctly, hire a neurotic. —Shara Hiner

~

I've concluded you are an eight ulcer man on four ulcer pay. —Harry S. Truman to Paul Hume, music critic, after his less than complimentary review of his daughter, Margaret's concert.

~

I have never yet met a healthy person who worries very much about his health, or a really good person who worries much about his own soul.
-J.B.S. Haldane, 1892-1964

~

The doctor who had treated an 80-year-old woman for most of her life finally retired. At her next checkup, the new physician told her to bring a list of all the medicines that had been prescribed for her. Looking over the list, his eyes grew wide as he found a prescription for birth control pills. "Mrs. Smith, do you realize these are birth control pills? "Yes, they help me sleep at night," said Mrs. Smith. The doctor said, "Madame, I assure you there is absolutely nothing in them that could possibly help you sleep!" She reached out and patted the young Doctor's knee. "Yes, Dear, I know that. But every morning, I grind one up and mix it in the glass of orange juice that my granddaughter drinks, and I'll tell you, it helps me sleep at night. —Unknown

~

If you want to test your memory, try to remember what you were worrying about one year ago today.
-E. Joseph Cossman

~

At a psychiatrist's conference on anxiety, one of the speakers said, "Anyone who isn't tense these days probably isn't well."

~

Those of us who live on the cusp of joining a coronary and ulcer club should learn a lesson from the dogs! Physicians and psychologists who do research in ulcers have stopped doing experiments with dogs. The reason is dogs don't have enough ambition or self-motivation. If you inflict an ulcer upon a dog, it will just lie around until it is cured. It refuses to worry about it. -Bits and Pieces

~

I've tried relaxing, but I feel more at home when I'm tense. –Unknown

~

Historian Arnold Toynbee used Jesus' words from Matthew, "Do not think that I've come to bring peace on earth; I have not come to bring peace, but a sword" to illustrate that throughout history, tension comes to a society whenever a creative genius steps forward with a new or revolutionary idea. Some resent a creative genius. Others welcome him or her.

BIRTH

It sometimes happens, even in the best of families, that a baby is born. This is not necessarily cause for alarm. The important thing is to keep your wits about you and borrow some money.
–Elinor Goulding Smith

~

The Scottish Presbyterian Church once banned anesthesia for its women members who were in labor believing that pain in childbirth was God's will.

~

There are two beginnings to every person's life. The first is the day one is born. The second is the moment when one discovers *why* one was born.

~

In a Sunday school class the subject got around to kindness to animals and the teacher thought it helpful to ask the children to talk about their pets. "I have a brand new dog", ventured a small boy. "What kind of dog is it?" asked the teacher. "Oh, it's a mixed up kind--- sort of a cocker scandal."

~

"Give me a sentence about someone whose work helps others," said a teacher. The child answered, "The fireman came down the ladder pregnant." The teacher took the boy aside to correct him. "Don't you know what pregnant means?" she asked. "Sure, I do", said the boy confidently. "It means carrying a child."

~

There are no illegitimate children—only illegitimate parents.
Leon Yankwich, US District Court Judge

~

"Mother, how was I born?" "How did I get here?" "The stork brought you, honey," she said. "Well, how about Bobby?" "The stork brought him too," she replied. "How about our cousins, Sally and Gretchen, did the stork bring them too?" "That's right," Mamma exclaimed. Said the child, "Gosh, Mom, we haven't had a normal birth in years, have we?"

~

"One Hundred Years of the American Novel"
1856: She has canceled all her social engagements
1880: She is in an interesting condition
1895: She is in a delicate condition
1910: She is knitting little booties.
1920: She is in a family way.
1935: She is expecting.
1956: She is pregnant.
(Today: She's going to have a baby.)
-Harry Golden. *For 2 Cents Plain*

~

The cause of death is birth. –George Harrison of The Beatles

~

James Atwood

Everything takes practice, except being born. -Sharon Mathews

~

In her poem, "Christmas Comes", Ann Weems reminds us that no one can stop a birth.

Christmas comes every time we see God in other persons.
The human and the holy meet in Bethlehem or in Times Square,
For Christmas comes like a golden storm on its way
To Jerusalem—
Determinedly, inevitably. . .
Even now it comes
In the face of hatred and warring—
No atrocity too terrible to stop it,
No Herod strong enough,
No curse shocking enough,
No disaster shattering enough—
For someone on earth will see the star,
Someone will hear the angel voices,
Someone will run to Bethlehem,
Someone will know peace and good will:
The Christ will be born."

~

After a Christmas when the children received lots of presents, one remarked, "I sure hope Joseph and Mary have another baby next year."

~

A little girl wrote a letter to God. . . "Dear God, I read the Bible. What does begat mean? Nobody will tell me."

~

"Daddy, where did I come from?" asked the boy. The father told him much more than he really wanted to know. "Does that answer your question, son?" "I guess so, dad. Billy said he was from Iowa City."

~

Two sisters were looking at a painting of the Virgin Mary and the infant Jesus. "But, where is Joseph?" asked the younger. "Silly, he's taking the picture," the older replied.   -James Dent, Charleston, WV, "Gazette"

~

A man spoke frantically into the phone. "My wife is pregnant and her contractions are only two minutes apart." The doctor asked, "Is this her first child?" "No", the man shouted, "I'm her husband."

~

Chuck Nevitt, a North Carolina State University basketball player, was nervous at practice. He explained his condition to his coach, Jim Valvano. "My sister is expecting a baby and I don't know whether I'm going to be an uncle or an aunt."

~

Everybody has a belly button except Adam and Eve.

~

Our four year old grandson, Oliver, was explaining belly buttons to his cousins. "Our belly buttons are what's left of a cord that went from our mother's stomach into our stomachs when we were inside our mommy's tummies. We were fed through the cord and that's how we could grow. But when we were born, the doctor cut the cord. "Why did he do that?" they asked. "Well, if he didn't cut it, we'd have to drag our mothers with us everywhere we went."

~

If nature had arranged that husbands and wives should have children
alternatively, there would never be more than three in a family.
-Laurence Housman

~

Our birth is nothing but our death begun,
As tapers waste the moment they take fire.
-Edward Young

~

We have been God-like in our planned breeding of our domesticated plants and animals, but we have been rabbit- like in our unplanned breeding of ourselves.   -Arnold Toynbee

~

The hungry world cannot be fed until and unless the growth of its resources and the growth of its populations come into balance. Each man and woman-- and each nation-- must make decisions of conscience and policy in the face of this great problem.   -Lyndon Baines Johnson

~

A flirtatious middle-aged man sidled up to a pretty young woman and said, Hi, beautiful! Where have you been all my life?" She replied, "Well, sir, for the first half of it, I wasn't even born."

~

Yes, I believe in life after death. But more importantly, I believe in life after birth.

~

Jean Henderson was the first woman ordained by the Beavers Butler Presbytery in America. When her first baby was due, a resolution was sent giving her permission to "labor within the bounds of the Presbytery".

~

The proud young mother had just returned from the doctor's office where she had paid something on her account. "Just think, Honey," she said to her husband, "only four more payments and the baby is ours."   -Paul Holdcraft

~

"What's your birthday?" a man asked his middle-aged woman friend. "July 26th," she replied. "What year?" he asked again. "Every year," she replied.

~

Stop crime at its source. Support Planned Parenthood. –Robert Byrne

~

CHRISTMAS

The mother told her neighbor, "We were visited by a round, jolly bearded man on Christmas Eve who came into the house with a huge pack on his back... my son brought home his laundry from college."

~

Christmas is the only time all year when we stare for days at a dead tree and eat candy out of our socks.   -Unknown

~

Our problem is not getting Christ in Christmas. Our problem is getting Christ in ourselves. It is plainly a matter of permitting Christmas to do something to us rather than covering it up with a carnival of jolly paganism."   -Donald McCleod

~

Imagine waking up one cold December morning in Davenport, IA, ready to hear beautiful Christmas carols on the radio only to be greeted with the strains of, "Grandma Got Run Over By A Reindeer." It played not once or twice, but twenty-seven straight times. The disc jockey, John Daniels, was depressed because of a snow storm. It took the station manager three hours to get to the station and get Daniels off the air.   -UPI, 12/19/85

~

Dorothy Fisher wrote a beautiful Christmas story in which the little boy, David, was in his back yard standing in the snow and looking up into the December sky as the stars came out. His mother had never seen him so quiet. She tiptoed to his side and found him mumbling to himself as little children often do. He said, "Just look at all those stars. They shine so bright but they don't make a sound." His mother saw in his face the miracle of an awakening soul. After a long pause, David says, "You know, Mom, I thought I could hear those stars singing." The wise men did too.

~

Recently I received a haunting Christmas postcard. It read: "A modest proposal for Christmas: "Be it resolved, the Christians of the world will not kill one another."

~

According to the Rev. James A. Simpson, there are three periods in a person's life:
1. When you believe in Santa Claus
2. When you don't believe in Santa Claus
3. When you are Santa Claus

~

With the billion dollar toy industry running at full speed, it's no wonder that one commentator spoke of the three wise men journeying to Jerusalem with their gifts of gold, frankincense, and an I-pod.

~

A friend watched a co-worker in his office who boasted of being an atheist, happily prepare an elaborate Christmas letter to send to family and friends. He asked, "How come, you, an atheist, are sending a Christmas greeting?" The person replied, "Christmas is a pagan holiday that you Christians have taken over. I'm just taking it back."

~

Christmas is over. Uncork your ambition.
Back to the battle! Come on, competition.
Down with all sentiment, can scrupulosity.
Money is all that is worth all your labors;
Crowd your competitors, nix on your neighbors.
Frenzy yourself into sickness and dizziness-
Christmas is over and business is business.
-Franklin Pierce Adams

~

Bulletin blooper for the Christmas Season:
Hymn: *I Heard the Bills on Christmas Day*

~

Rev. Ukai, Pastor of the Ginza Church in Tokyo, was decorating the entrance of the church for the Christmas season. A friendly bar-maid, who worked in the neighborhood, walked by. When she saw him happily decorating the church she inquired, "Oh, do you celebrate Christmas too?"

~

Every year I asked our youngest children in Sunday school to draw their interpretations of the manger scene. We then copied their drawings on the bulletins for Christmas Eve. One of my favorites pictured the stable with a big sign on top and an arrow pointing down. The sign read, "Right here".

~

I brake for Christmas.   --Bumper Sticker

~

In 1994, an individual doing research about Christmas sent out thousands of letters which included a "No Postage Necessary" postcard for the requested information. One was returned with this scrawled message: "We're not Christians. Kindly keep Jesus to yourself. . . Merry Christmas."

~

Grandma took her granddaughter for a shopping trip in the mall and promised her before they returned home they would see Santa Claus. After the little girl sat on Santa's lap and told him her heart's desire, the jolly old man gave her a candy cane. Grandma, standing by the exit, said, "What do you say to Santa, honey?" She looked back and said in a happy voice, "Charge it."

~

The first and most serious problem on Christmas morning: the batteries are not included.

~

Make this a Christmas your spouse won't forget. Charge everything.
–Sign in department store

~

Marj Carpenter, former moderator of the Presbyterian Church, USA, kept a doll from her childhood which she called, "Buttercup." She kept it in the attic and brought it out every year at Christmas to be the baby Jesus in the manger. But she had to explain herself when one of her kids told another, 'The baby Jesus lives at our house. We keep him in the closet until Christmas.'

~

Starbuck's Coffee announced it had dropped its suit against a Baltimore, MD, company for selling "Christmas Blend Coffee." They previously claimed a trademark for the name, but a judge ruled that no one owns Christmas.   -NPR. 2-5-98

~

Attending our first Christmas pageant in Tokyo we were startled with the wise men that were played by three little boys in academic gowns and mortar boards. Is there a better way for the East to show their esteem for wisdom?

~

The Supreme Court has ruled against a nativity scene in Washington, DC, this Christmas season. The ruling is not based on church/state issues, but is simply pragmatic. Officials have not been able to locate three wise men and a virgin in the nation's capitol. However, they found plenty of asses to fill the stable.

~

On Christmas Day, 1914, only five months into World War I, German, British, and French soldiers, already sick and tired of the senseless killing, disobeyed their superiors and fraternized with "the enemy" along two-thirds of the Western Front (in times of war, a crime punishable by death). German troops held Christmas trees up out of the trenches with signs, "Merry Christmas." "You no shoot, we no shoot." Thousands of troops streamed across a no-man's land strewn with rotting corpses. They sang Christmas carols, exchanged photographs of loved ones back home, shared rations, played football, even roasted some meat. Soldiers embraced men they had been trying to kill a few short hours before. They agreed to warn each other if the top brass forced them to fire their weapons, and to aim high.

A shudder ran through the high command on both sides. Here was disaster in the making: soldiers declaring their brotherhood with each other and refusing to fight. Generals on both sides declared this spontaneous peacemaking to be treasonous and subject to court martial. By March 1915, the fraternization movement had been eradicated and the killing machine put back in full operation. By the time of the armistice in 1918, millions would be slaughtered. Not many people have heard the story of the Christmas Truce. Military leaders have not gone out of their way to publicize it. The Christmas Truce story goes against much of what we have been taught about people. It gives us a glimpse of the world as we wish it could be. The Christmas Truce reminds us "This really happened once." It's like hearing that our deepest hopes can come true. The world really could be different.   -Excerpted from David G. Stratman, *We CAN Change the World: The Real Meaning of Everyday Life* (New Democracy Books, 1991).

~

Many of us can identify with Gillian in John Van Bruten's play, "Bell, Book, and Candle." Someone said to her, "Darling, you're depressed." Gillian replies, "I know, it must be Christmas. It always upsets me."

~

"UNPLUG THE CHRISTMAS MACHINE"

~

It is good to be a child sometimes and never better than at Christmas when its mighty Founder was a child himself.
                                                                    -Charles Dickens

~

During the 1930's Thelma Goldstein from Chicago took her first vacation in Florida. Being unfamiliar with the area, she wandered into a "restricted hotel" in Miami Beach. Approaching the desk, she said,

My name is Thelma Goldstein and I'd like a small room for two weeks.

Desk clerk: All of our rooms are booked. (Just as he said this, a man came down, put his key on the counter and checked out.)

Thelma: What luck, now there's a room.

Desk clerk: I'm sorry but this hotel is restricted. No Jews allowed.

Thelma: Jewish? Who's Jewish? I happen to be Catholic.

Desk Clerk: I find that hard to believe. Let me ask you who was the son of God?

Thelma: Jesus, Son of Mary

Desk Clerk: Where was he born?

Thelma: In a stable.

Desk Clerk: And why was he born in a stable?

Thelma: Because a schmuck like you wouldn't let a Jew rent a room in his hotel.

~

In a small town in the Midwest, the trash collectors attach a Christmas card to the garbage cans. "Seasons Greetings from your trash collector." The clients usually respond with a monetary gift. Recently, they have started a new tradition by attaching to the garbage cans another card, "Seasons Greetings from your trash collector. FINAL NOTICE."

~

Tonight, for the first time, the prison gates have opened.
Music and sudden light have interrupted our routine tonight,
And swept the filth of habit from our hearts.
–W.H. Auden "A Christmas Oratorio"

~

Christmas is the time when mothers and wives separate the men from the toys.

~

Christmas is that time of the year when you buy this year's presents with next year's money.
                                                                    –Bob Phillips

~

COMFORT

A woman was dreading her 7:30 operation. The aide arrived at 10:30, to take her to the operating room. "You're three hours late. They must be mighty busy this morning," she ventured. The aide sighed, "Oh, lady, you don't know the half of it. It's a zoo around this place today. We don't know whether we're coming or going. People are dying like flies today. Are you ready?"

~

A little girl on the way to nursery school told her mother she was going to be sad today. The mother asked why. She replied, "Because that's when the teacher let's you sit on her lap."

~

A young mother received a telephone call informing her that her mother had died. She hung up the phone, sat down on the couch, and wept. Her two year old daughter saw her distress and wanted to help. She sat down bedside her mother and began to pat her leg. When that didn't seem to help she went to her bedroom, brought her comfort blanket and said, "Here Mommy."

~

The ad immediately caught my attention: **Lay down your arms.** *Ah, to read without aching arms and dented elbows. Now you can, with our readers' table from Denmark, get rid of aching arms and dented elbows. It adjusts easily to hold your book at just the right height and angle. Reading becomes surprisingly comfortable in a chair, in bed, or beside a desk. An intelligent design and a handsome piece of furniture in teak, mahogany, cherry, oak, or black ash. (I didn't realize one could even get a dented elbow or that it could be such a problem.)*   *-The New Yorker*

~

A woman was ill and unable to attend church. She sent her nine year old son and instructed him to listen carefully and tell her what the sermon was all about. On returning home, he told his mother that the subject was, "Don't worry, you'll get the quilt." She asked him to repeat that, which he did, but it didn't make sense. Puzzled, she called the preacher and asked him to tell her the subject of the sermon. He replied that his key text was, "Fear not. The Comforter will come."

~

My pickup truck has an extended cab. One can put a lot of stuff where the "jump seats" are. The problem is it's impossible for even a small child to *sit* on the seats for a short time without getting gangrene. Nevertheless, in front of each jump seat is a cup holder. Isn't that thoughtful!

~

A mother kissed her daughter goodnight and was about to go back downstairs, but the little girl clung tightly to her and would not let her go. "But, sweetheart, you have your doll, and God is with you." "Yes," said the little girl, "I know I have my doll, and I know that God is with me, but I need somebody with a real skin face."

–Unknown

~

One night I dreamed I was walking along the beach with the Lord. Many scenes of my life passed across my mind. In each scene I noticed footprints in the sand. Sometimes, there were two sets of footprints; other times, only one. This bothered me because I felt that during the low periods of my life, when I was suffering from anguish, sorrow, or defeat, I could see only one set of footprints. I said to the Lord, "You promised me, Lord, if I followed you, you would walk with me always. But during these most trying times of my life, there was only one set of footprints in the sand. Why, when I needed you most, have you not been there for me?" The Lord replied, "The times when you have seen only one set of footprints, my child, is when I carried you." -Unknown

~

There are few scenes in literature more moving than the fourth act of Henry V. In the English camp at Agincourt, King Henry has fielded a poor, war-torn army that is shivering around its campfires, waiting to be slaughtered by the French at dawn. Henry V goes out to visit his men. As he walks about the camp, his men "pluck comfort from the cheerful semblance and sweet majesty of their leader" so that in the morning they have courage to do battle as new men because they have known "a little touch of Henry in the night."

~

It's not so much our friend's help that helps us as the confident knowledge that they will help us. -Epicures

~

A group, all of Scottish ancestry, gathered for a cruise on Lake Michigan. Most of the women went on deck and most of the men went below. When the breeze kicked up and it got cold topside, one of the women shouted down below, "Have you got a mackintosh or two down there to keep some of us warm?" There was a slight pause, broken by one of the enterprising Scotsmen who said, "We don't have a mackintosh, but we've got a McMillan and a McIntyre down here who are willing to give it a try." -Unknown

~

An Alfred Williams tells of an old lady who sat in the front of their church. Each Sunday she would hold the minister's hand at the door after the service and say, "Mr. Scott, that was a beautiful sermon." If the sermon was lacking in quality she would identify some part of the service: "Mr. Scott, that was a beautiful prayer." She always found something nice to say. But one Sunday everything seemed to go wrong. He had had an exceptionally busy week and had been up all Saturday night trying to reconcile a divided family. That day she took his hand, looked up and said, "Mr. Scott, that was beautiful text."

~

Beware of ministers who offer the comfort of opinion without the discomfort of thought. –Herb Meza

~

Harold McKeithen confessed to one of his parishioners that his sermon was too long. An elderly woman and faithful supporter overheard his lament and chimed in, "Oh, Harold, it wasn't too long. It just seemed long."

~

DECISION

We know what happens to people who stay in the middle of the road. They get run over.
-Aneurin Bevan

~

If someone tells you he is going to make a "realistic decision", you immediately know that he has resolved to do something bad.   –Mary McCarthy, *On the Contrary*

~

My grandfather returned from the Illinois State Fair to his home in Cherry Valley and quickly saddled his horse. He rode off to Rockford to gain counsel from his trusted friend, the banker. At the fair, stock was offered in a new company for $1.00 per share and he was considering investing the $1000 he had saved, but he needed sound advice. He asked his friend if the Ford Motor Car Company might be a good investment. The expert's reply was, *"Why, Jim, nothing will ever take the place of the horse and buggy."* Unfortunately, my grandfather listened to the expert.

~

Neutral men are the Devil's allies.   –Edwin Chapin, US clergyman, 1814-1880

~

An Indian chief was telling a story to the children of the village one night around the fire. He told them of the good wolf and the evil wolf which lived inside of him. He said, "Every day they fight and tear at each other. The good wolf wants me to be happy, do loving things, give hope to the people, and to be compassionate to my enemies." The evil wolf is angry and full of bad thoughts about everything. He wants me to be mean and selfish; he is angry and full of hate. Every day the good wolf and the evil wolf fight each other. The children listened with rapt attention wondering what would happen to the two wolves. Finally, one of the youngest children asked, "Grandfather, who wins, the good wolf or the evil wolf? After a pause the old man looked deep into each of the children's eyes and said, *"which ever one I feed."*
-Anonymous

~

The world is very different now. For man holds in his mortal hands the power to abolish all forms of human poverty and all forms of human life.
--John F. Kennedy, nomination acceptance speech, 1960

~

There was a little boy in the nursery whose major problem was deciding whether he would rather be a man or a woman when he grew up. Day after day this little fellow would balance the relative advantages of being the father or the mother in the family and he'd decide now for one and then for the other. But, some day this little boy will discover that his options are not as extensive as he first supposed.
–Unknown

~

In Holman Hunt's famous picture of "The Light of the World," Jesus stands knocking at the door with a lantern in his hand. If you look closely you find that the door has no handle. Whether or not Jesus gets inside is dependent on the person on the other side of that closed door. She can open to the light of the world or stay in her own darkness.

~

One is not required to respond to the impulse to be kind. One can always reject it. Maxim Gorky tells a revealing story of taking Lenin at the height of the Civil War to hear a young Russian pianist. Among other pieces he played was Beethoven's *Appassionata Sonata*. Lenin was greatly moved and said how much he deplored the fact that he lived at a time in history when he was forced to be cruel. "As long as this war lasts I will not listen to any more such music," he lamented."

~

A man went to an ice cream stand and asked what flavors they had. The young fellow behind the counter said in a raspy, weak voice, "Vanilla, chocolate and strawberry." The gentleman said, "You must have laryngitis." "Never heard of it," said the man, "all we've got is vanilla, chocolate and strawberry."

~

The final choice, of course, is between two countries from which no traveler returns: Heaven for climate. Hell for society.   –Mark Twain

~

Once the egg is scrambled you can't change your mind.

~

You don't get to choose how you're going to die, or when. You can only decide how you're going to live NOW!   -Joan Baez

~

During the Eisenhower administration, Charles Wilson, the secretary of defense, leaked the news that he had a good job in the Pentagon for just the right man. The only requirement was that he be a one-armed man. Pressed for an explanation, Wilson said, "I'm surrounded by people who give me advice and say, 'On the one hand, you ought to do this; but on the other hand you ought to do that.' I'm in great need of a one-armed man."   -"Minneapolis Tribune"

~

I made up my mind. But I made it up both ways.   -Casey Stengle

~

When you come to a fork in the road, take it.
-*Yogi Berra, upon receiving a Doctorate of Humanities, Montclair University, 1966*

~

Dante's *Inferno* tells it like it is: The hottest corners of hell are reserved for those who, during a moment of crisis, maintain their neutrality.

~

If people don't want to come to the ball park, nobody's gonna stop them.   –Yogi Berra

~

When Leo Durocher was the manager of the New York Giants, the owner of the team, Horace Stoneham, paid a visit to the dugout. In a dicey situation, Leo turned to his boss and asked, "What would you do here?" Stoneham said, "Let me think for a second." Durocher replied, "Too late."

~

In a day of illusion and utter confusion,
upon our delusion we base our conclusion.
-Author Unknown

The undecided could go one way or another. —President George W. Bush

~

After a battle is over, people talk a lot about how decisions were methodically reached, but actually there's always a hell of a lot of groping around.

—Frank Jack Fletcher

~

If you are interested in setting up a good stereo music system in your home, do you *really* want to go to a sophisticated electronics store that offers approximately 6.5 million options? Going to a cell phone company only requires you to choose one of 200 different packages.

~

When I read his license plate I immediately felt a strong kinship. It read: "PLAN B."

~

It does not take much strength to do things, but it requires great strength to decide on what to do.   —Elbert Hubbard

~

The margin of a single vote has been responsible for many of the great decisions, victories, defeats and disappointments of history.

Thomas Jefferson was elected President by one vote in the Electoral College. So was John Quincy Adams. Rutherford B. Hayes was elected President by one vote. His election was contested; referred to an electoral commission; the matter was again decided by a single vote. The man who had cast the deciding vote for President Hayes was himself elected to Congress by a margin of one vote. That one vote was cast by a voter who, though desperately ill, insisted on being taken to the polls.

Marcus Morton was elected governor of Massachusetts by one vote. Countless mayors, legislators, councilmen, and other public officials have enjoyed the sweet wine of victory or the bitter gall of defeat by a single vote. California, Washington, Idaho, Texas and Oregon gained statehood by one vote.

The ill-considered War of 1812 was brought about by a series of events based upon a single vote.   —J.M. Braude

~

DESPAIR (Depression)

A Methodist pastor was concerned about a disheveled old man who always stood outside the barbershop looking as if he didn't have a friend in the world. The pastor's heart went out to him. After getting a haircut one afternoon, he approached the man and said, "Don't Despair," and handed him two dollars. A few days later as he walked by the shop, the old man reached out, pulled him close and pressed a ten dollar bill in his hand. "What's this?" inquired the minister. "Don't Despair," he said. "He won yesterday at Santa Anita—paid 5 to 1."

~

When my high school sweetheart ended our romance, I went home and tried to go to sleep. I tossed and turned. Then, I went to the refrigerator and cut a piece of watermelon, ate it and went back to bed. I tossed and turned some more and went back to the fridge and cut another piece of watermelon. Once again, I tried in vain to go to sleep. I ate the whole watermelon. That gave me *two* reasons to stay up all night.

~

The husband was grumpy for days on end. His wife says: "You always complain about being depressed but you insist on reading world news."

~

The secret of being miserable is to have the leisure to bother whether or not you are happy.   -George Bernard Shaw

~

I date myself and at the same time feel sorry for the younger set who never had the pleasure of reading the Burma Shave limericks which dotted American highways of the 50's and 60's. One of my favorites was "Train approaching- Whistle screaming – Stop- Avoid that run down feeling."   -Burma Shave.

~

From the gutter to you ain't up. –Song Title

~

Being sad in the presence of Jesus is an existential impossibility.   -Schillenbeck

~

The best bridge between despair and hope is a good night's sleep.
--E. Joseph Cossman

~

After the trauma of September 11, 2001, I kept repeating three words over and over again: "Oh, my God! Oh, my God! Oh, my God!"

~

Despair: The eclipse of God. –Martin Buber

~

When you are down in the mouth remember Jonah. He came out all right.
-Thomas Edison

~

In John Steinbeck's, *Travels With Charley*, he tells of an old Arab who gave him mint tea in a glass so coated with use that it was opaque, but who handed him companionship with the tea and the tea was wonderful because of it. Says Steinbeck, "Then I began to formulate a new law regarding despondency. A sad soul can kill you quicker, far quicker, than a germ."

~

In Gail Sheehey's book, *Passages,* an individual confessed to her that she was not able to discover a real purpose for her life. "I've always used my work as a substitute for solving problems in my life. It began when I married. I packed my life with activity in order to avoid major personal decisions. What I do is give up autonomy by creating a high demand situation so that I must always jump from project to project, never really allowing time to think about why I'm doing it. Since I turned 40 it's become clearer to me that the reason I do this is I really haven't wanted to scrutinize what my life is all about." Then a measure of hope creeps in as she says, "Just the idea of stopping to investigate it is an indication that something has changed."

~

The mass of men lead lives of quiet desperation. What is called resignation is confirmed desperation. . . . A stereotyped but unconscious despair is concealed even under what are called the games and amusements of mankind.

—Henry David Thoreau

~

In a moment of supreme happiness Robert Browning wrote:
>The year's at the Spring- and day's at the morn;
>Morning's at seven; the hillside's dew pearled;
>The lark's on the wing; the snail's on the thorn;
>God's in his heaven- all's right with the world.

But with a totally different outlook on life he had this to say:
>I give the fight up;
>Let there be an end, a privacy,
>An obscure nook for me.
>I want to be forgotten, even by God.

~

The old English preacher, J.H. Jowett, called on a cobbler whose house was in a small seaside village in northern England. The man worked in a small, dark room. Jowett asked him if he ever got depressed working in such a small, isolated space. The man replied, "Oh, no, if any feelings of that sort begin, I just open this door." His door opened to the living room which had a glorious view of the sea.

~

FEAR

TOO MANY PEOPLE ARE RUNNING FROM
SOMETHING THAT ISN'T AFTER THEM —

Linus said to Charlie Brown, "I don't like to face problems head on. I think the best way to solve problems is to avoid them. This is a distinct philosophy of mine. No problem is so big or complicated that it cannot be run away from.
-Charles M. Shulz, "Peanuts"

~

Nothing scares me more than scared people. –Robert Frost

~

Hoover Rupert, writing in "The Presbyterian Outlook", tells of his friend, Dr. Charles Fosberg's moment of fear. Dr. Fosberg awoke early one morning with a horrible awareness that somebody was standing right beside his bed. He was so sure of it he broke out in a cold sweat. Slowly he moved his hand toward the bedside lamp and, from somewhere, got the courage to turn it on. The previous day, Fosberg and his wife took their children to Disneyland and brought home a balloon. Before bedtime the children were playing in their bedroom and let go of the balloon's string so it clung to the ceiling. Dr. Fosberg had gone to bed without turning on the light and didn't notice it. During the night the helium leaked out and the balloon drifted down until it was at eye-level beside his pillow. When he turned on the light, expecting the worst, he was face to face with Mickey Mouse."

~

Let us be of good cheer, remembering that the misfortunes hardest to bear are those which never come.
-Amy Lowell, 1847-1925

~

You gain strength, courage and confidence by every experience in which you really stop to look fear in the face. . . *You must do the thing which you think you cannot do*
.
—Eleanor Roosevelt, *You Can Learn by Living*

~

When climbing a rickety stair to his execution, Sir Thomas More said to his attendant, "I pray you, see me safe up, and as for my coming down, let me shift for myself."

~

A man cut across a cemetery lot at night and fell in an open grave. He tried and tried to jump and claw his way out but to no avail. Then he heard noises. There was another fellow cutting through the cemetery. Sure enough he fell in the same grave. The first man hunched over in the grave said in a low voice, "Don't even think about getting out of here." But he did.

~

Yesterday upon the stair, I met a man who wasn't there.
He wasn't there again today. I wish that man would go away.   -Nursery rhyme

~

Fear is the enemy of learning; it gives ignorance its power.   -William Sloane Coffin

~

A farmer with his little dog beside him was driving his horse drawn cart back to the farm, when at the top of the hill a car swerved out of control and knocked the cart, the horse, the dog and the man into the ditch. The man was in great pain with two broken legs, two broken arms, and several broken ribs. Soon the sheriff came and walked over to the horse, shook his head, then took out his pistol and put him out of his misery. He then went to the dog, and seeing how badly the dog was injured, shot him too. Then, he bent down over the farmer and asked, "How are you, Sir?" The man replied, "Sheriff, I've never felt better in my life."

~

A man cannot at the same time be fearful for himself and considerate of his fellows. As Stevenson put it in "Aes Triplex," "The man who has the least fear for his own carcass has most time to consider others."

~

Death is not the enemy. Living in fear of death is the enemy.   –Norman Cousins

~

It is brave to be involved. To be fearful is to be unresolved.   –Gwendolyn Brooks

~

A pastor asked one of his eight year old members if he prayed at night. The boy replied, "Yep, every night." "Do you pray in the morning when you get up?" The child answered, "Nope, I'm not scared in the morning."

~

A four year old said to her mother, "Take my hand, mommy. As soon as we cross the street, I'm running away from home."

~

In the "War against Terrorism" Attorney General John Ashcroft issued these words in December 2001. "We have once again received credible reports that *more bad things* may occur somewhere at some indefinite point in the coming weeks, months, or possibly years. According to our intercepts, the color *blue* may somehow be involved. Citizens are advised to be on highest alert whenever they are in the proximity of the color *blue*. Of course, citizens should be aware that this may be a coded reference to some entirely different color, such as red, yellow or green, and should act accordingly. Finally, I would like to emphasize that, while further attacks could occur at any moment, without any warning whatsoever, and may be chemical, biological, nuclear, or something SO TERRIBLE it hasn't even occurred to us yet--**the important thing is to remain calm."**

~

The electric company aired some commercials to demonstrate the awesome power of electricity. One such portrayed a father and his young son standing near a transformer where there were millions of volts passing through. The little boy is heard to say, "Daddy, I'm afraid." And the father replies, "That's good, Son. That's good. I'm glad you're afraid of such power."

~

It is said that just before a battle, Michel Ney, French military leader in the First Republic Army, found his knees trembling. He looked down scornfully at them and said; "Shaking, are you? Well, you'd shake a whole lot more if you knew where I was going to take you in the next half hour."

~

ONCE FOR EVERY DAY OF THE YEAR THE BIBLE TELLS US 365 TIMES TO "FEAR NOT."

~

In June 2005, eleven year old Boy Scout Brennan Hawkins remained lost for several days in the wilderness of the Colorado mountains. His parents had taught him never to talk to strangers. When some strangers, who served as volunteers, came near, he hid. His fear of strangers almost cost him his life.

~

We are now free from that inordinate fear of Communism which once led us to embrace any dictator who joined us in our fear.
-Jimmy Carter, University of Notre Dame, May 23, 1977

~

An Arab folk tale relates that Pestilence once met a caravan heading to Baghdad. "Why must you go to Baghdad?" asked the chief. "To take five thousand lives," Pestilence replied. Returning from the City of the Caliphs, Pestilence and the caravan met again. "You deceived me," the chief said angrily. "Instead of five thousand lives you took fifty thousand lives." Replied Pestilence, "No, five thousand, and not one more. Fear killed the rest."

~

Fear: The tax conscience pays to guilt. - Bob Phillips

~

The right honorable gentleman has sat so long on the fence that the iron has entered his soul.   –David Lloyd George, on John Simon, Government leader

~

He has not learned the lesson of life who does not every day surmount a fear.
                                        -Ralph Waldo Emerson

~

One of the sailors in Herman Melville's *Moby Dick* said he was not getting into the whale boat with anyone who wasn't afraid of the whale.

~

Prior to leaving for New York City to see some plays, two women from Wilmington, NC, were cautioned about the dangers of the city, warned not to wear jewelry, speak to strangers, and advised if anyone gave them any trouble, they were to do exactly as they were told. They were scared to death. When they arrived in the city they went directly to their hotel, ate dinner and decided to return to their room. Just before the elevator doors closed, a large man got on accompanied by a big dog. When the dog grew restless his owner got irritated and shouted, "Sit." Immediately the women sat down on the elevator floor. The man was embarrassed. "I'm sorry," he said, "I was talking to my dog. Please stand up." The women immediately stood up. The next morning when they finished breakfast they went to pay the bill. The cashier said, "It's already been taken care of." "But, we don't know anybody in New York. Who could have paid?" asked the women. The cashier pointed to Reggie Jackson of the New York Yankees.

~

How does one kill fear? I wonder? How do you shoot a specter through the heart? Slash off its spectral head? Take it by the spectral throat?   -Joseph Conrad

~

There is nothing more dangerous than a powerful nation that is afraid.
                                    -Methodist Bishop Timothy Whitaker

FUTURE

I have seen the future, and it's much like the present, only longer.
--Dan Quisenberry, Kansas City Royals

~

The fortune teller in London lost a lot of business when someone stole her crystal ball. When asked about it, she replied, "I didn't foresee it."

~

Not long ago William Easum wrote a book entitled *Dancing With Dinosaurs*. His thesis is that the church is in danger of becoming a dinosaur. He promotes this idea because even though we live in a secular and unchurched world, the church continues to develop its ministries and programs as if we still lived in a churched society.

~

Most of our future lies ahead of us.   -Danny Crum, Louisville Basketball Coach

~

Alfred Nobel perfected the means to manufacture explosives which were widely used for waging war and killing. When an explosion in his factory killed his younger brother, the local newspaper assumed that Alfred, himself, was dead and wrote his obituary. The headline read, *"The Master of Death is Dead."* Seeing in print what his legacy would be, he rewrote his will and stipulated that the major part of his $9 million dollar estate be set up as a fund to establish yearly prizes for merit in physics, chemistry, medicine, physiology, literature, and world peace.

~

I never think of the future; it comes soon enough. --Albert Einstein

~

Someone unknown engraved on the wall of a 17th century church: "In the year 1653, when all things sacred throughout the nation were either demolished or profaned, Baronet Sir Robert Shirley, founded this church; whose singular praise it is to have done the best things in the worst of times and hoped for them in the most calamitous."

~

The future will be better tomorrow. —George W. Bush

~

You must say goodbye to some things you know in order to say hello to some things you don't"
-William Faulkner

~

Putting something away for a rainy day takes a longer spell of dry weather than it used to.
–Howard Kirksey

~

The trouble with our times is that the future is not what it used to be.
–Paul Valery

~

21

It's better to have a hen tomorrow than an egg today. -Thomas Fuller

~

Someone asked Frank Lloyd Wright which of his works would be his greatest. The famous architect, at the age of 83, replied, "My next one."

~

When Bishop O'Reilly came down to breakfast he looked awful. He attributed his condition to a nightmare. "I was in the Sistine Chapel with the Bishop's Select Committee to plan the First Vatican Council of the 22nd Century. The Pope was in the chair, when one of the Bishops asked, "Will those of us who are married be allowed to bring our spouses to the opening convocation?" The Pope responded, "Certainly, I plan to bring my husband."
                                                                            -Unknown

~

Manana is the busiest day of the week. --Spanish proverb

~

A real country bumpkin took his first trip to the big city. The day he was to return he was intrigued by a weight and fortune machine which promised, "Your weight and fortune for a quarter." He dropped in his coin and immediately a little card appeared: "Your name is John Jones. You weigh 178 pounds. You live in Fairfax and you are waiting for the 5:15 train." He was stunned but still skeptical. He waited a few minutes and snuck around the corner, came up behind the machine and once more stepped on the scale. Again the little card appeared with the same message: "Your name is John Jones. You weigh 178 pounds. You live in Fairfax and you are waiting for the 5:15 train." Still, John was not a believer. Noticing there was a novelty store across the street he bought a mustache and a pair of sunglasses, and again stepped on the weight and fortune machine. Out came the card, "Your name is John Jones. You weigh 178 pounds. You live in Fairfax and you fooled around till you missed the 5:15 train."

~

In a new world, you must first kill all the lawyers.
- William Shakespeare, *Richard, III.*

~

One of the greatest labor-saving inventions of today is tomorrow.   –Vincent Foss

~

Norman Cousins reminds us that *"we live in a world where the number one problem is the possibility of nuclear annihilation in our own generation. Sobering thought. And then he says the number two problem is that our best minds are not focused on the number one problem. We are committing, therefore, your children and your grandchildren's future to trusting, get this, trusting in a sinful, fallen humanity that they in turn would not make one mistake. Not one. We permit the world's future to hang by such a slender thread. I see that as utter confusion."*

~

The future has a way of arriving unannounced. -George Will

~

The trouble with the future is it keeps getting closer and closer.

~

HEY, YOU! .... OUT OF THE GENE POOL!   --Bumper Sticker

~

Back in the early days, Alton, MO, was earmarked for greatness and no one expected Saint Louis to remain anything but a sleepy little town. Some families in Saint Louis have preserved letters written to their ancestors that are addressed, *Saint Louis, near Alton."*

~

It's hard to predict the future. Adolph Hitler predicted his Third Reich would last 1,000 years. He was off by 988. George Custer said there would only be 300 Indians over that hill. He was 2,800 per cent wrong. The Captain of the Titanic, Edward J. Smith predicted that his ship would never sink. He was almost right. It only sank once. Thomas Malthus predicted that the population of the world was growing so fast that we'd all drive one another crazy by the end of the 19th Century. He was wrong. It didn't happen until last year. William Everett was another fuzzy forecaster. He ran the Patent Office in the early part of this century and predicted that it would soon close because everything worth while had already been invented. A few of the inventions he missed were TV, jet planes, the computer, micro wave ovens, telephone, space; to name a few."

-Robert Kirby, Chairman, Westinghouse Electric

~

For the aged, the future is today.   —Jerry Smart

~

When Bob Dole was running for President in 1996, a reporter asked, "Tell me senator, what is the essence of your campaign?" Dole replied, "It's about the future. That's where we're headed."

~

The debt that each generation owes to the past must pay to the future.
--Abigail Scott Duniway, 1834-1915

~

The life you have led doesn't need to be the only life you'll have. -Anna Quindlen

~

"When people say, 'She's got everything,' I have only one answer, 'I haven't had tomorrow.'"
-Elizabeth Taylor

~

A short fortune teller at the local jail escaped. The newspaper reported, "Small medium at large."

~

I'm not a has been. I'm a will be. -Lauren Bacall

~

It's tough to make predictions, especially about the future. —Yogi Berra

~

The Sunday school teacher was telling how Lot's wife looked back and turned into a pillar of salt. Little Johnny interrupted. "That makes sense to me. My mom looked back once when she was driving the car and turned into a telephone pole!"

~

GIFT (Generosity)

We sing about this so-called "true love" each Christmas. But I don't think he's deserving of the title. To the contrary, his gifts on the twelve days of Christmas tell me he has no sensitivity at all. Where, for example, are those milk maids, pipers, dancing ladies, leaping Lords, and twelve fiddlers going to have lunch? There are fifty of them, count 'em. What about their bathroom privileges during the holidays? And speaking of bathroom privileges, can you imagine what the front lawn is going to look like? I presume the milk maids brought their cows. Together with the swans, the geese, and calling birds, the French hens, the turtle doves, and the partridge, the front yard will be "ripe." The only things this so called "true love" gave his sweetheart that didn't cause some grief were the gold rings. And did she really need five of them? He wasn't a true love. A "true love" offers a gift that is needed.

~

What would happen if we did the unexpected this Christmas and paid less attention to the wrapped packages under the Christmas tree, and paid more attention to the gift of God wrapped in swaddling cloths and lying in a manger?

~

One reason people divorce is they run out of gift ideas. -Robert Byrne

~

24

Looking for a Christmas gift? In 2004, The DuPont and Robb Report advertised a lovely hand made chess set from Faberge for only 12.5 million. Coming down the scale, they had a nice Lamborghini Roadster for a mere $320,000. And for those of you whose ship has not yet come in, a fine golf cart is available for a paltry $15,000. Now, that's 2004 prices understand. Look them up on the web and I'm sure they'll send you a current catalog.

~

At a craft fair near Christmas I spoke with an artist who formerly was a Jehovah's Witness. Because they frown on gift-giving, Christmas was always a difficult time for her. It wasn't because she didn't receive gifts, but because she couldn't give any.

~

Cathy and Andrea are discussing the Christmas gifts they have purchased for family and friends. Cathy says to Andrea, "I've almost finished my Christmas shopping, Andrea!" Replies her friend, "Me too, Cathy, isn't it a great feeling? Luke and I made a contribution to the animal shelter for the Lerners. We adopted a sea lion at the zoo for the Dales. Wrote a check to fight against global warming for the Burkoffs, and sent food baskets to the homeless in the names of all our other friends!" The last scene pictures Cathy at the Customer Service Desk at the department store. She says, "Hello, I'd like to return 14 dancing flowers."

-Cathy Guisewite, "Cathy"

~

It's much better to give than to receive and it's deductible. –Unknown

~

At Christmas we speak often of the wise men and the gifts they brought to the Christ child. A little girl in Sunday school, who had recently become the big sister of a baby brother, commented, "Well, I guess the gold and all that other stuff was all right, but, I'll bet Mary wished someone had brought her some diapers."

~

One of my favorite Christmas gifts of all time was when I opened a note from my son and daughter.
"This paper is good for one afternoon of leaf raking next fall.
Love, Mebane and David."

~

The kindergarten child told his grandfather about the gifts the wise men brought the Christ child: "gold, common sense and fur."

~

Dr. William Rothwell of Pawtucket, RI, always paid the check when he ate with friends. He loved to be generous. He chose as his tombstone a big rock inscribed, "This one's on me."

~

No one is honored for what one has received.

~

Some people think they are generous because they give away free advice. –Unknown

~

An artist was asked for a contribution to his church's building fund drive. He said, "I can't give you a cash gift, but I can give you one of my paintings, which is worth seven to eight hundred dollars." Two weeks later, the chairman of the committee informed the artist that the church was still several hundred dollars short of its goal. "Well, change the worth of my painting to a thousand dollars," said the artist.

~

Two baggage handlers at the airport were talking about the best tippers. One said, "It's hard to say, but you should try and avoid the preachers." He continued, "We had a preacher's convention here last year. They came with the Ten Commandments in one hand and a five dollar bill in the other. When they left town, they hadn't broken either."

~

If you have no charity in your heart, you have the worst kind of heart trouble.
-Bob Hope

~

Generosity in life is a very different thing from generosity in the hour of death; one proceeds from genuine liberality and benevolence, the other from pride or fear.
-Horace Mann

~

Dr. Roy Angel of Central Baptist Church in Miami, FL, told of a member whose brother gave him a brand new car for Christmas. One afternoon the man left his office to drive home and found a little boy, in tattered clothes, stroking and admiring his car. When he put his key in the door lock, the child asked, "What's a car like this cost, mister?" He said, "Well, I really don't know. My brother gave it to me." The boy was stunned and asked, "You didn't pay nothin' for it? Your brother gave it to you?" "That's right. My brother gave it to me." He replied, "Gee, I wish I could be a brother like that!"

~

As a fifth grader I was in love with Lona Lee. It was Christmas time and we exchanged presents. I put hers under the tree and squeezed it daily to try and guess what was inside. On Christmas morning, I opened her gift and then my world fell in. She gave me a beautiful leather wallet and belt. I wondered if I could ever face Lona Lee again? I gave her a bar of soap. It was no ordinary bar of soap, mind you. It was made in the form of a Santa Claus and had a string on it which you could put around your neck in the shower. As soap goes, it was special, but it was still a bar of soap. Christmas afternoon, I walked the streets of Detroit to find a store which was open so I could buy something else for Lona Lee and even things up.

~

We'd all like a reputation for generosity and we'd all like to buy it cheap.
–Mignon McLaughlin

~

GOVERNMENT

After winning his first election to Washington, Harry Truman said he spent six months wondering how he made it to the Senate and the rest of his term wondering how his colleagues made it.

~

I would have made a good Pope. -Richard Nixon

~

This nation was conceived in liberty and dedicated to the principle—among others—that honest men may honestly disagree; that if they all say what they think, a majority of the people will be able to distinguish truth from error; that in the competition of the market place of ideas, the sounder ideas will in the long run win out. (Every now and then I have hope this is still true.)

–Elmer Davis, American writer, 1890-1958

~

It is dangerous to be right when the government is wrong. –Voltaire

~

"A good man can do nothing in office because the system is against him -- and a bad one can't do anything for the same reason. So as bad as we are, we are better off than any other nation."

-Will Rogers

~

A government which robs Peter to pay Paul, can always count on Paul's support.

--George Bernard Shaw

~

When the author Kurt Vonnegut and a friend returned from Europe following their service in World War II, Vonnegut asked his friend what he had learned from his wartime experiences? His friend replied: "Not to believe my government."

~

I don't make jokes. I just watch the government and report the facts.   -Will Rogers

~

We have a crisis of leadership in this country. Where are the Washingtons, the Jeffersons and the Jacksons? I'll tell you where they are. They are playing professional football and basketball. –Unknown

~

The problem with government is it scratches where there's no itch.   -Unknown

~

The only thing that saves us from the bureaucracy is its inefficiency.

-Eugene McCarthy

~

What luck for rulers that people do not think.   –Adolph Hitler

~

As a boy I was told anybody could become President. Today I **know** that's true.

~

The budget should be balanced, the treasury should be refilled, the public debt should be reduced, the arrogance of officialdom should be tempered and controlled. The mob should be forced to work and not depend on government for subsistence.
                                                                    --Cicero, 50 B.C.E.

~

When he emerged from Constitution Hall, Benjamin Franklin was asked by a woman, "What kind of government are you giving us?" He replied, "A republic, Madam, if you can keep it."

~

Man is the only animal that laughs and has a state legislature.   -Samuel Butler

~

Every decent man is ashamed of the government he lives under.   -H.L. Mencken

~

Democracy is the worst form of government except for all the others that have been tried.
                                                                    -Winston Churchill

~

Ninety percent of the politicians give the other ten percent a bad reputation.
                                                                    --Henry Kissinger

~

It's too bad that the people who know how to run the country are busy teaching school and driving taxi cabs.   –Unknown

~

I think the American public wants a solemn ass as president and I think I'll go along with them.   -Calvin Coolidge

~

There is no distinctly American criminal class, except Congress.   -Mark Twain

~

Govern a great nation as you would cook a small fish…don't overdo it.   --Lao-Tsze

~

If men were angels, no government would be necessary. If angels were to govern men, neither external nor internal controls on government would be necessary."
                                                                    –James Madison

~

The State… it is I. -Louis XIV of France

~

Themistocles said, "The Athenians govern the Greeks; I govern the Athenians; you, my wife, govern me; your son, governs you."
                                                                    –Plutarch

~

An ambassador is an honest man, sent abroad to lie for the good of his country.
                                                    -Sir Henry Wotton, British diplomat, 1604

~

The best way to protect the Constitution is to understand it.
                    -Foundation for the US Constitution

~

He mocks the people who propose that the government shall protect the rich that they in turn may care for the laboring poor.   – President Grover Cleveland

~

My experience in government is that when things are non-controversial and beautifully coordinated there is not much going on.   –President John F. Kennedy

~

You can have wealth concentrated in the hands of a few or democracy, but you can't have both.   – Supreme Court Justice Louis Brandeis

~

On March 1st, 2006, in Annapolis, MD, at a hearing on the proposed Constitutional Amendment to prohibit gay marriage, Jamie Raskin, professor of law at American University, was requested to testify. At the end of his testimony, Republican Senator Nancy Jacobs said: "Mr. Raskin, my Bible says marriage is only between a man and a woman. What do you have to say about that?" Raskin replied: "Senator, when you took your oath of office, you placed your hand on the Bible and swore to uphold the Constitution. You did not place your hand on the Constitution and swear to uphold the Bible."

~

All free governments are managed by the combined wisdom and folly of the people.   - James Garfield

~

About the time our original 13 states adopted their new constitution, Alexander Tyler, a Scottish history professor at the University of Edinburgh, had this to say about the fall of the Athenian Republic some 2000 years prior: "A democracy is always temporary in nature; it simply cannot exist as a permanent form of government. A democracy will continue to exist up until the time that voters discover they can vote themselves generous gifts from the public treasury. From that moment on, the majority always votes for the candidates who promise the most benefits from the public treasury, with the result that every democracy will finally collapse due to loose fiscal policy, which is always followed by a dictatorship."

"The average age of the worlds greatest civilizations from the beginning of history, has been about 200 years. During those 200 years, these nations always progressed through the following sequence:
1. From bondage to spiritual faith;
2. From spiritual faith to great courage;
3. From courage to liberty;
4. From liberty to abundance;
5. From abundance to complacency;
6. From complacency to apathy;
7. From apathy to dependence;
8. From dependence back into bondage. "

~

HISTORY*

I know people who can tell you in laborious detail about their ancestors who lived 200 years ago but have no clue where their kids were last night.

~

Our ignorance of history makes us libel our own times. People have always been like this.
-Gustave Flaubert

~

The three great elements of modern civilization are gunpowder, printing, and the Protestant religion.
-Thomas Carlyle, Scottish Historian, 1795-1881

~

History repeats itself. That's one of the things wrong with history.
-Clarence Darrow

~

History is the sum total of things that could have been avoided.
- Konrad Adenauer

~

Most of us spend too much time on the last 24 hours and too little on the last six thousand years.
-Will Durant

~

A short summary of every Jewish holiday: "They tried to kill us, we won, let's eat." -
Unknown

~

In George Bernard Shaw's *The Devil's Disciple,* Swingdon asks Burgoyne: What will history say? Burgoyne replies, "History, Sir, will tell lies as usual."

~

Sometimes theologians are naive about social science and especially about history. They act as if 'once upon a time' there were parishes that were perfectly organized to fulfill God's purposes and that only today they are failing. I know a magazine that has a standard answer when people write in and say, 'Your magazine is not as good as it used to be.' The editors write an answer, 'You are right. It never was.' So with the Parish. It never was "as good as it used to be."
-Martin Marty

~

Political history is too criminal a thing to teach children. --W.H. Auden

~

Few things happen at the right time and the rest do not happen at all. The conscientious historian will correct these defects.
--Herodotus, 400 B.C. E.

~

History never looks like history when you are living through it. It always looks confusing and messy and it always feels uncomfortable.
–John Gardner

~

* See *TIME*

Don't brood on what's past, but never forget it either.   --Thomas Raddall

~

HISTORY ISN'T OVER.
–Unknown

~

More history is made by secret handshakes than by battles, bills, and proclamations.   -John Barth

~

History is something that never happened, written by a man who wasn't there.
-Anonymous

~

Human history becomes more and more a race between education and catastrophe.   –Herbert Wells, Historian

~

God cannot alter the past but historians can. –Samuel Butler

~

His ear is so sensitively attuned to the bugle note of history that he is often deaf to the more raucous clamor of today.   –Winston Churchill of an opponent

~

What men learn from history is that men do not learn from history.   –Unknown

~

We will be remembered not for the power of our weapons but for the power of our compassion, our dedication to human welfare.   -Hubert Humphrey

~

The history of things that didn't happen has never been written. –Henry Kissinger

~

Even the gods cannot change history. -Agathon, 448-400 BCE

~

History, n. An account mostly false, of events mostly unimportant, which are brought about by rulers, mostly knaves, and soldiers, mostly fools.
-Ambrose Bierce

~

Traditionalists are pessimistic about the future and optimists about the past.   – Lewis Mumford

~

What is history but a fable agreed upon. – Napoleon

~

Those who make history don't have time to write it. – Metternich

~

History is nothing but a pack of tricks we play upon the dead. - Voltaire

~

HOPE*

Charlie Brown, bat and glove in hand, heads off for the baseball diamond. "I'm really looking forward to our game today. I just hope it doesn't rain." But, as the rain starts to fall, he laments, "I can't even hope good."

-Charles M. Shulz, "Peanuts"

~

Pope Pius V, on his death bed, cried out: "When I was in a low condition I had some hopes of salvation. When I was advanced to Cardinal I greatly doubted, but since I became a Pope I have no hope at all."

~

If one really believes in God, not in a theoretical analysis of deity, but in a basic fact which makes the universe moral through and through, then he may be sure that ought and can are twins.　　　–Harry Emerson Fosdick

~

During the Second World War everyone was straining their necks to get a look at President Roosevelt as his motorcade passed. A young father held his daughter on his shoulders so she could see the President as he sped by. Climbing down from her perch she remarked, "Pshaw, he's just a man."

~

If there is a sin against life, it consists perhaps not so much in despairing of life as in hoping for another life and in eluding the implacable grandeur of this life.

-Albert Camus

~

Gabriel Marcel, the Christian existentialist philosopher, writes, *"Optimism is possible as a constant attitude only when people isolate themselves from the real evils and obstacles of the world. On the other hand, the person who hopes is fully aware that sin abounds. In order to hope, one must know what it means to fear, to doubt, and to despair. True Christian hope is born in the pits when there's no where else to look, but up. Christian hope is born when we no longer look for human solutions to bring us a future. Christian hope is born when we're worn out with looking for yet some other way to save ourselves. Christian faith is born in the pits."*

~

An African American minister in the District of Columbia told of a burial he had for a teenager in his congregation who was shot and killed. He was a member of a gang and the gang members were his pall bearers: all thirteen of them. Each had a hand on the casket. You know, it usually takes just six, but here were 13 young men carrying the casket of their friend to its final resting place. When they reached the grave site, they bowed their heads for a moment of silence, and the leader said, "Jamie, we'll see you soon, buddy."

~

* See also PROVIDENCE

I am the poor white, fooled and pushed apart,

I am the Negro bearing slavery's scar,
I am the Red man driven from the land,
I am the immigrant clutching the hope I seek—
And finding only the same old stupid plan
Of dog eat dog, or might crush the weak.
O, yes,
I say it plain,
America never was America to me
And yet I swear this oath—
America will be!
--Langston Hughes, American poet

~

Hope criticizes what is, hopelessness rationalizes it. Hope resists, hopelessness adapts.
–William Sloane Coffin

~

Everybody said Robert Ingersoll was an infidel. But would a person bereft of hope speak as he did at his brother's grave? *"Life is a narrow vale between the cold and barren peaks of two eternities. We strive in vain to look beyond the height. We cry aloud and the only answer is the echo of our wailing cry. From the voiceless lips of the unreplying dead there comes no word. But in the night of death hope sees a star and listening love can hear the rustle of a wing."*

~

Hope is the feeling that the feeling you have isn't permanent. -Jean Kerr

~

Said Margaret Mead, the great anthropologist, *"Human beings reach their greatest heights when their deepest values are most endangered and most in need of defense and fostering. In times of crisis, human beings know that they must put forth greater efforts and so greater efforts are forthcoming."*

~

Everything that is done in the world is done by hope. -Martin Luther

~

HOPE IS PATIENCE WITH THE LAMP LIT. –Tertullian

~

THERE IS NEVER SO MUCH FALSE HOPE AS IN THE FIRST SIX HOURS OF A DIET.
–Unknown

~

The Christian hope is an incautious and extravagant hope. But in such a place as this, in a world that so regularly winds our clocks and breaks our hearts that laughs at caution and cries from every corner for extravagance—only outlandish hopes can make themselves at home.
-Robert Farrar Capon

~

Hope is the confusion of the desire for a thing with its probability.
–Arthur Schopenhauer 1788-1860

~

What a great line Mary Martin sang in the musical, *South Pacific*, "I'm stuck like a dope with a thing called hope, and I can't get it out of my life."

~

George Watts portrays the struggle for hope in this world in his painting called, "Hope". It shows a dejected woman sitting atop the globe of the world with her back bent as though every muscle had surrendered to awful circumstances. Her eyes are sorrowful as she clutches a lyre whose strings are broken. One wonders why the picture is not called, "Despair" instead of "Hope". Yet, there is *one* string on the lyre which is not broken. On seeing this picture, Harold Beglie wrote this poem, which captures the Biblical meaning of hope.

> *One star, one string, and all the rest*
> *Darkness and everlasting space,*
> *Save that she carries in her breast*
> *The travail of the race.*
>
> *Born thro' the cold and soundless deep*
> *Of ruin riding in the air,*
> *She bows, too heavenly to weep,*
> *Too human to despair.*
>
> *And ever on her lonely string*
> *Expects some music from above,*
> *Some faint, confirming whispering*
> *Of fatherhood and love.*
>
> *One star, one string, and through the drift*
> *Of eons, and with human cries,*
> *She waits the hand of God to lift*
> *The bandage from her eyes.*

~

"What did you do today, Tommy?" the father asked his ten year old son. "We played baseball. We're behind 23-0," he said. The father replied, "Gee, Son, I know you're disappointed. It's hard to lose like that." Tommy looked up at his Dad and said, "I know it's bad, Dad, but we haven't batted yet."

~

> Hope is the thing with feathers
> That perches in the soul
> And sings the tune without the words
> And never stops at all.
> –Emily Dickinson

~

HOSPITALITY

"NEVER MISTAKE ENDURANCE FOR HOSPITALITY!"

After a nice visit with one of his elderly parishioners, the gentleman said, "Pastor, since it is difficult for me to get to church, why don't I write a check which will fulfill my pledge for the year. I'll go get my checkbook." While he was gone, the pastor helped himself to the peanuts in the dish on the coffee table. When the man returned, he said, "I'm so glad you're enjoying those peanuts. You know, with my dentures, all I can do is suck the chocolate off of them."

-"Context"

~

"Be not forgetful to entertain strangers: for thereby some have entertained angels unawares."

-Hebrews 13:2

~

A young student minister from Georgia arrived at one of his members homes at 5:00 PM. The woman of the house said, "Didn't I tell you to come after supper?" "Yes, you did. That's why I'm here!"

~

Nowhere does the Torah say, Invite your guest to pray; but it does tell us to offer a guest food, drink, and a bed.

–Jewish Proverb

~

In Victor Hugo's book, *Les Miserables*, the escaped prisoner Jean Valjean was looking for understanding and love wherever he could find it. One rainy night, cold and wet, he went from house to house but was turned away. In despair he sat down and complained to a passer by that he had knocked on every door in town and been turned aside. The man asked, as he pointed to the church, "Have you knocked on that door?"

~

My first summer assignment while in seminary was at the First Presbyterian Church of Statesville, NC. As a young bachelor I was often invited to eat in the homes of the congregation. One particular family served a delicious southern fried chicken dinner with rice and gravy, butter beans, corn and all the trimmings. I was seated beside the grandfather who was a very friendly old gentleman and without a tooth in his head. He took it upon himself to see that "the preacher" had enough to eat.

I had almost finished what was on my plate when he said, "Preacher, have some more chicken." After I took a piece, he said, "You'll need some more rice and gravy." He put his spoon in his mouth and licked it clean; stirred the rice and gave me several spoonfuls. Again, he said, "Have some more butter beans." He licked clean his spoon once more and served me some beans. I knew from that moment on that in the ministry, there would always be folks who would see to it that I had enough to eat and they would serve me with a clean spoon.

~

Not only our society, but even Jesus' church, is hesitant to fully welcome our homosexual brothers and sisters. We tell so many, "Please don't be honest with us. Please keep quiet. We don't know who you are, but we know you're out there somewhere, even very close by, but we must not know **who** you are. Please don't tell us. If you are honest with us, we will have problems. If you tell us who you really are, we won't know how to welcome you. Please stay in the closet and bear the shame society says you should bear. When I was a boy growing up in Detroit, that's the way we treated families who had a retarded child and were reluctant to talk about it with their neighbors. "Shhh", we whispered. Keep it quiet. Keep them in the house. Don't tell anyone, just shut the door."

~

When Walter Frere was bishop of Truro, a vicar invited him to stay the night after a Confirmation. Before supper, Frere was walking down a dimly-lit passage in the Vicarage when the vicar's wife, coming up from behind, gave him a clout over the ear, with the remark: That'll teach you to ask the bishop to stay when we've nothing in the house!

- Ronald Brown, bishop of Birkenhead

~

Humankind is divided into two great classes: hosts and guests.
– Sir Max Beerbohm, 1872-1956

~

Be content with whatever you have, and do not get a name for living on hospitality.
–Ecclesiasticus 29:23

~

HUMILITY

My opponent is a very humble man and he has much to be humble about.

-Winston Churchill

~

An interesting spiritual exercise might be for each of us to **think humbly and realistically about our own importance in the world.** Believing in the sovereignty of Almighty God and the Lordship of Jesus Christ, we might ask ourselves, "Is there any person, church, company, organization, or country so dependent on *one* human being whose knowledge or power is so great that it would mean disaster if that one person were not available? It might help each of us to consider that things might be even better if some of us were not around. The graveyards are full of "indispensable" people.

~

Upon the highest throne in the world, we are seated still, upon our own arses.

- Michel de Montaigne

~

In October of 1967, a guide was showing me around Yong Nak Presbyterian Church in Seoul, Korea, that was then the largest Presbyterian Church in the world. As we walked through the basement I heard a piano and some singing which was terribly off key. I thought to myself, I've never heard such awful music. I asked about it and the guide replied, "I'll show you." He opened a door to a special class for deaf mutes who were standing around the piano singing hymns of praise to God. The longer I listened, the more pleasing the music became. Of one thing I have no doubt. It was beautiful music to Almighty God who listens regularly to the best of the heavenly choirs.

~

Prior to the experience above, I had been occasionally chastised for choosing a hymn or two, which were not familiar to the congregation. Some would even get angry and say, "I couldn't sing the hymns today. I didn't know the tune." Then I would get that mea-culpa hang-dog look, exhibited by most clergy. Nowadays, having heard deaf mutes sing their praise to God, I pay little attention to those who can't sing the hymns because they don't know the tune.

~

We hear a lot these days of the importance of assertiveness training. Certainly, some folks need to take it, but wouldn't the world be better off if there were lots of classes offered in HUMILITY TRAINING. As I observe the world situation, our major problems are not because we hold *too low* an opinion of ourselves.

~

Heard at a prayer meeting before worship: "God, just take our preacher this morning and just blot him out."

~

A man who had just been promoted to vice president of his company boasted so much about it that his wife finally said, "Vice presidents are a dime a dozen. Why, I'd bet that even Albertson's has a vice president in charge of fruit. " The husband called Albertson's just for spite and asked to speak to the vice president in charge of fruit and the operator asked, "fresh or dried?"

~

I just said I was the greatest. I never thought I was. –Muhammad Ali

~

In Alan Paton's book, *Ah, But Your Land Is Beautiful,* he tells the true story which comes out of the racial unrest of South Africa. The racial tension had risen to a new high and the Rev. Isaiah Buti, pastor of the Holy Church of Zion, paid a visit to Judge Jan Christian Olivier, who, as a white leader, had great sympathy for the black cause. He asked the judge to participate in the foot washing service at the church on Good Friday.

Buti said there will be three people who will have their feet washed. "I will wash the feet of an elderly member. Her daughter will wash the feet of a disabled person. And then, he said, "I'm going to ask you, Judge Olivier, to wash the feet of Martha Fortuin."

Paton writes, "The judge answered, "Why, she's washed the feet of all of my children many times. Why should I not wash her feet?" Then Buti instructed the judge to come after the service had started and wait in the back of the church. So, on Good Friday, Judge Olivier goes to the Holy Church of Zion and waits in the back of the room so as not to be noticed, until Martha Fortuin, who had worked for him for years, is called forward. With head downcast as becomes a modest and devout woman and conscious of the honor that had been bestowed on her, she goes forward. The Rev. Buti calls out the name of Jan Christian Olivier, and though Martha was silent, she heard the gasp of the congregation as the great respected Judge walked up to her to wash her feet. The Rev. Buti gave the towel to the judge and he, as the Word says, girded himself with it, takes the dish of water and knelt at the feet of Martha Fortuin. He took the right foot in his hands, washed it and dried it with the towel. Then he took her other foot in his hands, washed it and dried it with the towel. Then he took both of her feet tenderly, because they were tired from much serving, and kissed them both. Then Martha Fortuin and many others in the Holy Church of Zion fell weeping in that holy place.

~

After worship a woman came to the door and said, "You were marvelous this morning." The pastor said, "You know it wasn't me. It was the Lord." Replied the woman, "Oh, you weren't that good."

~

Swallowing one's pride never choked anyone.

~

I feel coming on me a strange disease -- humility.
--Frank Lloyd Wright on receiving the Gold Medal of the National Institute of Arts and Letters.

~

Corrie ten Boom was once asked if it was difficult for her to remain humble. She replied, "When Jesus rode into Jerusalem on Palm Sunday on the back of a donkey and everyone was waving palm branches and throwing garments in the road and singing praises, do you think that for one moment it ever entered the head of the donkey that any of that was for him? If I can be on the donkey on which Jesus Christ rides in his glory, I give him all the praise and all the honor."
–Stephen Gauhroger, A-Z Sparkling Illustrations

~

Two generals with several inches of medals on their broad chests were walking down the halls of the Pentagon. One told the other about his nightmare: "I tell you, Stan, it was awful. I dreamed that the Bible was right and the meek really *are* going to inherit the earth."

~

According to one authority in Washington, things are getting so bad that the meek don't even want to inherit the earth.

~

William Beebe, the naturalist, used to tell of a ritual he and Teddy Roosevelt had during the summer at Sagamore Hill. After an evening of talk, the two would go out on the lawn and search the skies for a certain spot of star- like light beyond the lower left-hand corner of the Great Square of Pegasus. Then Roosevelt would recite: "That is the Spiral Galaxy of Andromeda. It is as large as our Milky Way. It is one of a hundred million galaxies. It consists of one hundred billion suns, each larger than our sun." Then Roosevelt would grin and say, "Now I think we are small enough! Let's go to bed."   -Quoted by Harry Emerson Fosdick

~

I used to think that God's gifts were on shelves one above the other and that the taller we grow in Christian character, the more easily we should reach them. I find now that God's gifts are on shelves one beneath the other and that it is not a question of growing taller, but of stooping lower, always lower, to get God's best gifts.   -F. B. Meyer

~

A veteran British diplomat had a favorite way to put down a pushy or egotistical junior. The diplomat would call the younger man in for a heart- to- heart talk and quite often at the end of the talk would say, 'Young man, you have broken the fifth rule: You have taken yourself too seriously.' That would end the meeting— except that invariably, as the younger man got to the door, he would turn and ask, 'What are the other rules?' And the diplomat would smile serenely and answer, 'There are no other rules.' "   -John Chancellor

~

Don't be humble. You're not that great. -Golda Meir

~

After a long and flattering introduction, the speaker for the evening said, "I feel like the fly that was smashed on my windshield. I didn't know I had so much in me."

~

If we don't learn to be meek there will be no earth for anyone to inherit.

~

When Mahatma Gandhi was leading the people of India in their struggle against colonialism, a wealthy Brahman offered his services to Gandhi. He thanked him and then sent him out to clean toilets. The gentleman requested a private meeting with his leader and complained, "Sir, I have a Ph.D. from the London School of Economics, why have you sent me out to clean the toilets? I can do great things for you." Gandhi replied, "I know you can do great things, but I did not know if you could do small things."

~

I have been selected to fill an important office for a brief period, and am now, in your eyes invested with an influence which will soon pass away; but should my administration prove to be a very wicked one, or what is more probable, a very foolish one, if you, the people, are but true to yourselves and to the Constitution, there is but little harm I can do, thank God.   -Abraham Lincoln on himself. Feb. 12, 1861

~

Ebrahim Samba directs the World Health Organization's river blindness project in West Africa which is credited with helping to save the lives of more than 30 million people. When asked if he had a secret weapon, he said: I got down on my knees and prayed. We tend to give human beings all the credit for accomplishments, but we are merely instruments, put here to seek and do God's will. Truly, if the larvae of a single little fly can cause enough river blindness to wipe out an entire village, who do you think you are?"

~

Several years ago a young college girl visited Beethoven's home and asked permission to play his piano. After playing a few bars she mused to the guard, "I suppose all the great musicians ask to play on this piano during their visits." He replied, "No. Paderewski was here two years ago and said he was not worthy to touch Beethoven's piano."

~

The windows of my house are small but they look out on a large world. –Chinese Proverb

~

The humility which consists of saying you are of little worth is not Christian humility. It is one form of self-occupation and a very poor and futile one at that.

—William Temple, *Christ in His Church*

~

Humility: The first of all other virtues for other people. –Oliver Wendell Holmes

~

INCARNATION*

"I SAY IF WE BELIEVE IN INCARNATION
WE OUGHT TO FIX THE SEWERS "

A parish priest in London was asked why he, as a Christian minister, should have so much to say on the improvement of the sewers in the slums of London. He replied, "Because I believe in the incarnation." (John Calvin faced the same criticism and gave the same answer.)

~

Jesus reached out and touched the leper and his leprosy was gone. He could have spoken the cure as he did on other occasions. Yet, could he? *In that particular situation?* Could he really cure a leper with only a word? Love, in this instance, required more than a word. It was necessary to touch a man who hadn't been touched in months, perhaps years. Love, for *this man* required skin on skin. Love required that Jesus break the rules and regulations of his society. Jesus crossed the chasm of the law. Love couldn't heal at arm's length.

~

From a collection of the lives of the saints of Islam comes this story which concerns King Ebrahim. He was very wealthy and wanted desperately to know God. One night the King was roused from sleep by a fearful stomping on the roof above his bed. Alarmed, he shouted out, "Who's there?" "A friend," came the reply from the roof. "I've lost my camel." Perturbed by such stupidity, Ebrahim screamed out, "You fool. Are you looking for a camel on the roof?" The voice from the roof answered, "You are the fool. Are you looking for God in silk clothing, lying on a golden bed?" These words so spoke to King Ebrahim that he gave away much of his wealth and went on to become a remarkable saint.

~

* See also *JESUS*

By virtue of the creation and, still more, of the incarnation, nothing here below is
profane for those who know how to see.
-Pierre Teilhard de Chardin

~

"Daddy, Where Was God?"

Daddy, where was God? Where oh where, was God when the rural police broke
down the fence, burned the hut, destroyed the crops, killed the pigs, raped
Imelda, and ate up our guavas?
He was up there, Son. He was up there.
Daddy, where was God? Where, oh where was God when, because we
complained, the judge came from town to fine us, and......
He was up there, Son.
Daddy, where, oh where was God when in our absence the cornfield
dried up, just like Imelda dried up, the baby got whooping cough and
grandmother had a fever?
He was up there, Son
Daddy, then we have to tell God clearly that He has to come down from
time to time to be with us. Daddy, you see how we are, without crops, hut,
pigs, without anything, and God, God does nothing. It's not fair, Daddy.
If God is really up there-- let God come down and be with us in this
unbearable hunger. Let God come down to sweat in the cornfield; let God
come down to be in jail; let God come down to spit stones in the hands of the
sold out judge and the rural police who rob and kill the campesinos.
-Vinicio Jose Aguilar wrote this poem to show the suffering of the Latin-American Christian community.

~

Beware of the man whose god is in the skies. -George Bernard Shaw

~

The Creator of the spheres went to the back door to a barn that may have been
the only place in town where there was any room for the birth of a poor baby
named Jesus. The Eternal slipped into our humanity that night on an unnamed
side street in Bethlehem. God came in the back door of history as a member of a
dispossessed minority in a forsaken corner of the world called Palestine. When
the one who set the stars in their orbits steps into our town today, He does not
automatically come first to Herod's Palace, or the White House, or Jerusalem
Estates or the houses on Country Club Drive. The Savior comes first to those who
confess their deep need for a visit from the Savior. No wonder the appearance of
such a One is so startling and surprising. How on earth can we prepare for the
Advent of such a One as this?
-Milton S. Carothers, sermon fragment

~

JESUS*

Mary Glover, an elderly Pentecostal Christian in Washington, DC, prayed this prayer every day as the homeless received their meal at a soup kitchen just a short distance from The White House: "Lord, we know that you'll be comin' through this line today, so Lord, help us to treat you well."

~

Christ cannot possibly have been a Jew. I don't have to prove that scientifically. It is a fact.   -Joseph Goebbels, Hitler's Propaganda Minister

~

The minister asked the children, "What is gray, has a fluffy tail, eats nuts, and climbs trees?" The children just sat there, not making a sound. The preacher couldn't figure it out. The question was simple enough. He repeated it: "What is gray, has a fluffy tail, eats nuts and climbs trees?" One little boy said hesitatingly, "Preacher, I'm sure that the answer is Jesus, but it sounds like a squirrel to me."

~

A pre-school was busy with Christmas preparations and making gifts for parents, painting cards, etc. When story-time came, the teacher of the three-year-old class was trying to lay some background for the story of Jesus' birth. However, Jennifer jumped the gun. She said, "You're talking about Jesus. I know who Jesus is. Jesus is the wayshore." The teacher was puzzled. She asked Jennifer, "Who?" and Jennifer answered, with a little irritation, "The Wayshore. Jesus is the one who shows us the way."   -"The Epistle", Central Presbyterian Church, Atlanta, GA

~

When the minister was talking to the children during worship he showed them a picture of Jesus and said, "This is not really Jesus. It's what the artist imagined Jesus would look like." That didn't translate for one little boy who said, "It sure looks like Jesus to me."

~

Albert Schweitzer concludes his book, *The Quest for the Historical Jesus* with these words: "He comes to us as One unknown, without a name, as of old, by the lake-side he came to those men who knew Him not. He speaks to us the same word: 'Follow thou me!' and sets us to the tasks which He has to fulfill for our time. He commands. And to those who obey Him, whether they be wise or simple, He will reveal Himself in the toils, the conflicts, the sufferings which they shall pass through in His fellowship, and, as an ineffable mystery, they shall learn in their own experience Who He is."

~

Those who search for the historical Jesus have looked and looked into a deep, deep well and what they discover is their own reflection.
                                                    -Reginald Fuller, New Testament scholar

~

* See also *INCARNATION*

On the day after Christmas, someone discovered the baby Jesus was missing from the manger scene at a San Francisco church. The police were called and they searched with no success. Finally someone spotted the statue in the back of a shiny red wagon being pulled by a young boy. The excited priest was informed that the boy had prayed for a new wagon for Christmas and had promised the little baby Jesus would get a ride if Santa brought the wagon."

-"Context"

~

Our problem is not getting Christ in Christmas. Our problem is getting Christ in ourselves. It is plainly a matter of permitting Christmas to do something to us rather than covering it up with a carnival of jolly paganism."   -Donald McCleod

~

A few years ago "Self Magazine" polled its readers to determine the most popular public heroes. Jesus made the list, but he came in behind Mother Teresa, George Bush, some generals and movie stars.

-Quoted in Donald W. McCullough, *The Trivialization of God*

~

I think Jesus would have been a great basketball player. He would have been one of the most tenacious guys out there. I think he'd really get in your face. Nothing dirty, but he'd play to win."   -Mark Eaton, Utah Jazz

~

One Solitary Life: Here is a man who was born and grew up in an obscure village, the child of a peasant woman. He worked in a carpenter shop until he was thirty years of age, and then for three years was an itinerant preacher. He never wrote a book. He never held an office. He never owned a home. He never had a family. He never went to college. He never put his foot inside a really big city. He never traveled more than 200 miles from the place he was born. He had no credentials but himself. While he was still a young man, the tide of popular opinion turned against him and he was turned over to his enemies. He went through the mockery of a trial. He was nailed upon a cross between two thieves. His executioners gambled for his only possession on earth, his seamless robe. When he was dead, he was taken down from the cross and laid in a borrowed grave through the courtesy of a friend. Twenty centuries have come and gone, and today Jesus is the centerpiece of the human race. All the armies that ever marched and all the navies that were ever built, all the parliaments that have ever sat, and all the kings that have ever ruled, put together, have not affected humanity like this one solitary life."   –James Allen Francis, 1928

~

Some amateur mountain climbers hired a strong, experienced guide in their attempt to climb a mountain. They soon came upon a chasm in the rocks that had to be crossed. Hundreds of feet below was the valley. The guide jumped the gap, grabbed hold of the rocks on the other side and stuck out his hand to pull the rest of the climbers across. They were afraid to reach out and take his hand. He said, "I've been this way before. Trust me. This is the only way up the mountain. Just take my hand. I've never lost anyone yet." Oh? And neither has Jesus, the Christ.

~

Phillips Brooks, the writer of the Christmas Carol, *O Little Town of Bethlehem*, had this to say about Jesus: In the best sense of the word, Jesus was a radical. . . His religion has so long been identified with conservatism: that it is almost startling sometimes to remember that all the conservatives of his own times were against him; that it was the young, free, restless, sanguine, progressive part of the people who flocked to him.

~

In the 1970's, one of my Japanese students, Hirotaka Kashiwase, sent me a post card after we had several conversations about Jesus Christ. *I attended the 12th World Baptist Congress at the Budokan in Tokyo. It was magnificent and dignified. I felt as if I were in another world. And who is Jesus Christ to me now? –The greatest and the most beautiful human being that ever existed--however, the weakest."* He was on to something wasn't he? We cannot, we dare not, forget that the Lord said, "I am meek and lowly in heart." He also said, "The meek shall inherit the earth." The young man mentioned above is today, Dr. Hirotaka Kashiwase, a psychiatrist in Tokyo. I trust that he is daily assuring his patients that *there is strength in gentleness.*

~

There are three good arguments that Jesus was Black:
    1. He called everyone "brother."
    2. He liked Gospel.
    3. He couldn't get a fair trial.
There are three equally good arguments that Jesus was Jewish:
    1. He went into His Fathers business.
    2. He lived at home until he was 33.
    3. He knew his Mother was a virgin and his mother knew he was God.
There are three equally good arguments that Jesus was Italian:
    1. He talked with his hands.
    2. He had wine with every meal.
    3. He used olive oil.
There are three equally good arguments that Jesus was a Californian:
    1. He never cut his hair.
    2. He walked around barefoot all the time.
    3. He started a new religion.
There are three equally good arguments that Jesus was Irish:
    1. He never got married.
    2. He was always telling stories.
    3. He loved green pastures.
But the most compelling arguments show that Jesus was a woman:
    1. He fed a crowd at a moment's notice when there was no food.
    2. He tried to get a message across to a bunch of men who just didn't get it.
    3. And even when He was dead, Jesus had to get up because there was more work to do.

– Anonymous

~

JOY (Happiness)

Success is getting what you want. Happiness is liking what you get.   –H. J. Brown

~

A happy man or woman is a better thing to find than a five pound note. He or she is a radiating focus of good will; and their entrance into a room is as though another candle had been lighted.   –Robert Louis Stevenson

~

I know some Christians who live with the haunting fear that someone, somewhere may be happy.   -H.L. Mencken's definition of Puritanism

~

There are four varieties of people; the lovers, the ambitious, observers, and fools. The fools are the happiest.   -Taine Hippolyte, 1823-1893

~

Happiness is an imaginary condition, formerly often attributed by the living to the dead, now usually attributed by adults to children, and by children to adults.
                    -Thomas Szasz

~

You can always spot a happy motorcycle rider by the bugs on his teeth.

~

When one considers the decisions we must make today, the most important question seems to be, "Am I going to enjoy it?" That has become the first priority. We are not asking, "Is it right?" "Is it good?" "Is it best for me, my family and my community?" but, "Is it going to be fun?"

~

Modern Americans travel light, with little philosophic baggage other than a fervent belief in their right to the pursuit of happiness.   –George Will

~

James MaGuire wrote in *Reader's Digest*: "As part of her pre-confirmation training, my daughter, Cathy, had to select a virtue she promised to work on. The virtue she chose was, "perseverance." Then she learned that she had to embroider that word on a sash for the confirmation ceremony. "I'm switching virtues, dad," Cathy informed me. "To what"? I asked. "To joy", she replied.

~

One can enjoy sorrow alone, but it takes two to be glad. -Elbert Hubbard

~

My son played strong safety in football. After a game in which he played particularly well, he came home all excited. "Dad, I want to tell you about the best feeling in the world. It's when a tight end comes across the line of scrimmage and lifts his arms up high for a pass, and you have a running start and hit him in the ribs with your helmet and you hear him say "Aaagh" and he goes down in a heap, writhing on the ground. Oh, Dad, it's such a great feeling!"

~

It's pretty hard to tell what brings happiness. Poverty and wealth have both failed.
-Kim Hubbard

~

Be happy while you're living; you're a long time dead. --Scottish proverb

~

The wedding was a week after the terrorist attacks on New York City and the Pentagon in September 2001. Hardly anyone was in a celebratory mood. But the bride's aunts and uncles came all the way from Sweden to attend the wedding. They acted as therapists as they reminded us that it was time to celebrate again. The song they taught us was so comforting and uplifting, especially the chorus: "BRAVO, BRAVO, BRAVISSIMO. HOORAY." It was time to celebrate love again, to rejoice in God's gift of marriage. It was time once more to enjoy the little children who danced at the reception. It's time to tell jokes again, to laugh again, to go to ball games and have picnics again. It's time to rejoice in the wonderful gifts of God: "BRAVO, BRAVO, BRAVISSIMO, HOORAY!"

~

I'm a Scotch Calvinist and nothing makes us happier than misery. –James Reston

~

Joy is knowing that you are the right person in the right place at the right time.

~

A Chinese emperor once asked a wise man to take a month and figure out the meaning of happiness. When he returned, the wise man said, "Happiness is when the grandfather dies, then the father, and then the son."

~

Happiness is like jam. You can't spread it without getting some of it on yourself.

~

Cheerfulness is contagious. But don't wait to catch it. Be a carrier.

~

I slept and dreamed that life was happiness. I awoke and saw that life was service. I served and found that in service happiness was found.
-Rabindranath Tagore, 1803-1882

~

Happiness is a way station between too little and too much. –Channing Pollock

~

If we'd only stop trying to be happy, we'd have a pretty good time.
–Edith Wharton

~

A person is happiest and most successful when dedicated to a cause outside his own individual selfish satisfaction.
-Dr. Benjamin Spock

Happiness is like a butterfly, which, when pursued, is always just beyond our grasp, but which, if you will sit down quietly, may alight upon you.
-Nathaniel Hawthorne

~

Happiness is nothing more than health and a poor memory.   –Albert Schweitzer

~

Mirth is God's medicine. Everybody ought to bathe in it. Grim care, moroseness, anxiety—all this rust of life--ought to be scoured off by the oil of mirth.
                                                                –Henry Ward Beecher

~

No matter what happens, someone will find a way to take it too seriously.   -Dave Barry

~

So why are Christians so often so joyless? I think it's because too often Christians have only enough religion to make themselves miserable. Guilt they know but not forgiveness.   –William Sloane Coffin

~

The man who is happy is not he who is believed to be so, but he who believes he is so.
                                    -Michel de Montaigne, 1553-1592

~

Frederick Buechner, in his book, *Whistling in the Dark: An ABC Theologized*, speaks about "jogger's high." *The look of anguish and despair that contorts the faces of most of the people you see huffing and puffing away at it by the side of the road, however, is striking. If you didn't know directly from them that they are having the time of their lives, the chances are you wouldn't be likely to guess it.*

~

Existence is a strange bargain. Life owes us little; we owe it everything. The only true happiness comes from squandering ourselves for a purpose.   –William Cowper

~

One thing I know: the only ones among you who will be really happy are those who will have sought and found how to serve.   –Albert Schweitzer

~

Happiness is seeing Lubbock, TX, in the rear view mirror.   –Song title

~

If there is no happiness on earth, the creation would be a monstrosity, and Voltaire would have been right when he called our planet the latrine of the universe.
              –Giacomo Girolamo Casanova de Seingalt, Ilalian Adventurer, 1725-1798

~

Whoever said money can't buy happiness didn't know where to shop.   –Bumper Sticker

~

I'm a kind of paranoiac in reverse. I suspect people of plotting to make me happy.
                        -J.D. Salinger

~

A man had been unhappy and tense for a long time. When he met his friend on the street, he had a smile on his face and a spring in his step. His friend asked, "John, what in the world has happened to you? You look wonderful." John replied, "Yesterday, I turned in my resignation as God's General Manager of the Universe."

~

JUDGMENT

Rufus Jones, the esteemed Quaker leader, tells of <u>his</u> judgment and conversion experience. His father died when he was very young, so he had to help his mother take care of the farm. One day he promised to pick the corn. But his friends came by with their fishing poles, heading for the river. "Come on Rufus, let's go fishing," they said. Rufus forgot about the corn. When he got home late that afternoon, his mother was picking the corn. She said, "Rufus, let's go to your room." He knew what was going to happen. He usually got a whipping when they went to his room together. But when they got there, she said, "Come on, Rufus, let's pray." They both got down on their knees beside the bed. His mother prayed: "Dear God, make a man out of Rufus. Amen." Then, his mother rose from her knees and left the room.

~

There are three inner circles in Hell where the flames are the hottest. One circle is for the fundamentalists who do not truly believe in the infallibility of the Scriptures. Another circle is for the Roman Catholics who do not really believe in the infallibility of the Pope. The third circle is for Episcopalians who pick up the wrong fork at dinner.

~

Moby Dick doesn't bite so much as he swallows. -Herman Melville

~

If a smoke detector buzzes in the middle of the night, it is a message that must be obeyed. Get out. The house is on fire. The message is not for contemplation on how hot it would be in the midst of the flame, or what damage might incur. Nor is it to consider that the buzzer has malfunctioned. If it goes off in the middle of the night, get up and get out.

~

"There's been a terrible mistake!" said the newest arrival in Hell. *"I was in Who's Who In American Colleges and Universities; I was a Phi Beta Kappa, a member of the New York Stock Exchange, and one of the 10 Best Dressed Men in America."*

~

Attending a dinner party one evening, the subjects of eternal punishment and eternal life came up. A heated discussion ensued, but Mark Twain said not one word. A woman sitting near him inquired, "What is your opinion, Mr. Twain, we'd like to hear from you." He replied, "Madam, please excuse me. I must remain silent. You see, I have friends in both places."

~

God says take what you want and pay for it. -Spanish Proverb

~

The price of wheat, wool, and corn go up and down, but the price of wild oats stays the same.
                                                                    -Anonymous

~

Rabbi Elimelech Lizensker said, "I am sure of my share in the world to come. When I stand to plead before the bar of the heavenly tribunal, I'll be asked, "Did you learn as in duty-bound?" To this I will make an answer: "No." Again, I will be asked, "Did you pray as in duty-bound?" Again my answer will be, "No." The third question will be: "Did you do good as in duty-bound?" And for the third time I will answer, "No." Then judgment will be awarded in my favor, for I will have spoken the truth.
-Hasidic story

~

I mistrust the judgment of every man in a case in which his own wishes are concerned.
-First Duke of Wellington

~

John Wesley tells of a man against whom year after year his irritability rose. He considered him covetous. One day he gave to Wesley a gift for one of his philanthropies; a gift which Wesley considered too small. Wesley condemned him vigorously. The man quietly said, "I know a man who at the beginning of the week buys a penny's worth of parsnips, takes them home and boils them and all week he has the parsnips for his meat and the water for his drink." "Who is the man?" Wesley asked. "I am," he replied. Wesley adds, "This he constantly did, although he had 200 pounds a year, that he might pay the debts he contracted before he knew God. And this was the man I considered covetous."

~

A businessman on vacation came across his own obituary in his home town paper. He was livid and called long distance to get the matter straight and make sure there was a speedy retraction. "I'm calling about the matter of my death which was reported in your Sunday paper." "Yes, sir," came the calm reply. "And just where are you calling us from, sir?"

~

The Scriptures say judgment begins with the household of God. We should therefore, listen to the word of the Psalmist, "[God will] accept no bull from your house." (Psalm 50:9 RSV) Unfortunately, scholars have once again tampered with the text. The NRSV renders the verse, "I will not accept a bull from your house." That's such a pity! *The text had such life in the RSV.*

~

On Judgment Day, at the last trumpet, the Lord will not send people to heaven or hell. He will take away their inhibitions so everybody can go where they belong.
-Edward F. Prichard, Jr.

~

At the day of judgment we shall not be asked what we've read, but what we've done.
-Thomas a Kempis

~

It is fair to judge people and stained glass only in their best light. -William Ward

~

I shall tell you a great secret, my friend. Do not wait
for the last judgment. It takes place every day. -Albert Camus

~

In 1975, Municipal Judge E.W. Thompson of Sulphur, LA, apologized for arriving in court ten minutes late and explained that a policeman had caught him driving 42 miles per hour in a 30-mile zone. When his own case came up on the docket, he stepped down from the bench, pleaded guilty, and fined himself $17.50.

-"The Prairie Overcomer." Paul Tan, *Encyclopedia of 7700 Illustrations*

~

Before returning to the United States after a trip to Martin Luther's Wittenburg, I ate breakfast with a group of pastors in Amsterdam. A colleague took more containers of jam than he could use and was about to throw them in the trash. I said, "Don't throw them out, I'll take them home." Upon arrival in New York, I was informed that KLM Airlines lost my bags and I was instructed to call them the next day. When I called collect, a woman said, "We don't accept collect calls." I told her since KLM lost my bags, they owed me the courtesy of accepting the collect call. Reluctantly, she accepted and asked me to describe my smallest bag and its contents. I replied, "I've been on a clergy trip to Eastern Germany and have a lot of papers and articles about Martin Luther." Coming back to the phone, she said, "Yes, reverend, It's all here, along with all the jam you stole from the hotel."

~

The preacher said on Judgment Day there will be earthquakes, fires and floods. That got the attention of a little boy. "Daddy, will we get out of school that day?"

~

The old Pentecostal preacher was preaching about Judgment Day and he cried out: "There will be weeping and gnashing of teeth. And them without teeth will have to gum it."

~

The mediaeval church socked it to its excommunicated sinners: Pope Clement VI (1478-1534) was especially unforgiving. "Let him be damned in his going out and his coming in. The Lord strike him with madness and blindness, May the heavens empty upon him thunderbolts and the wrath of the Omnipotent burn itself into him in the present and future world. May the universe light up against him and the earth open to swallow him up."

~

Do not judge God's world from your own. Trim your hedge as you wish and plant your flowers in the patterns you can understand, but do not judge the garden of nature from your own little window box.   — Georg Lichenberg 1742-1799

~

The preacher was telling the parishioners about the fires of Hell. "There will be weeping and gnashing of teeth", he said. One man said, "But, I don't have any teeth." Not to be outdone the preacher replied, "Don't worry about that, Sir. Teeth will be provided."

JUSTICE

Two businessmen are making plans. "Things aren't quite so simple anymore, Driggers. We will come out ahead if we pay more attention to justice matters."

~

Neither the Church of Christ nor a Christian commonwealth ought to tolerate such as prefer private gain to the public weal or seek it to the hurt of their neighbors.   --Martin Bucer, German Protestant Reformer, 1490-1551

~

The church is not called to be "merely a thermometer that records the ideas and principles of popular opinion, but a thermostat that transforms the mores of society."   -Martin Luther King Jr.

~

I should like to be able to love my country and still love justice.   -Albert Camus

~

A Mississippi Catechism (1857) to indoctrinate slaves reads:
    Q. Should servants ever run away?
    A. No. If they do, they sin against God and man.
    Q. How do you know this?
    A. The Bible tells us that the Apostle Paul found a servant who
    had run away from his master and he sent him home.
    Q. Why did not Paul conceal him, that he might be free?
    A. Because he would not make religion a cloak for injustice.
      -Marianne H. Micks, *Our Search for Identity*

~

Man's capacity for justice makes democracy possible; but man's inclination to injustice makes democracy necessary.   -Reinhold Niebuhr, Theologian

~

 It is wrong to say that God made rich and poor; God made only male and female; and God gave them the earth for their inheritance. . .The earth in its natural uncultivated state was, and ever would have continued to be, the common property of the human race.   −William Paley, Agrarian Justice, 1797

~

To show compassion for a person who is destitute and have little or no concern for the structures of society that make him needy is to be sentimental, not loving.

~

Write on my gravestone, "Infidel, Traitor"—infidel to every church that compromises with the strong; traitor to every government that oppresses the people.   -Wendell Phillips, American abolitionist, 1811-1884

~

"The Attorney General of the Unprotected and of the Friendless".
—Epitaph on the grave of William Wilberforce, Westminster Abbey

~

Learning that her husband had betrayed her, Vera Czermak jumped out of her third-story window in Prague. The Czech newspaper, *Vicerni Prahi*, reported that Mrs. Czermak was recovering in the hospital after landing on her husband who was killed.

~

Organized charity, scrimped and iced,
In the name of a cautious, statistical Christ.
--John Boyle O'Reilly, *In Bohemia*

~

The US Supreme Court ruled that the state of Missouri cannot discriminate against the Ku Klux Klan and deny it participation in the adopt-a-highway program. While seeing the name of the Klan on a highway sign is aesthetically disgusting, most realize that this decision is a victory for free speech and equal protection under the law. But, while the Department of Transportation in Missouri cannot remove the KKK's adopt-a-highway sign, the state does maintain the right to name the highway itself. The KKK has been cleaning up a stretch of the "Rosa Parks Freeway".

~

A Government to perform even a minimum of service to its people, must take steps to suppress avarice, to strike down privately built up schemes of economic exploitation or oppression, to uproot privilege, and to assure justice and economic opportunity to the masses. —Robert Jackson, US Supreme Court Justice 1892-1954

~

We're always saving someone afar off when the fellow beside us ain't eating.
-Will Rogers

~

The contemporary church is so often a weak, ineffective voice with an uncertain sound. It is so often the arch-supporter of the status quo. Far from being disturbed by the presence of the church, the power structure of the average community is consoled by the church's silent and vocal sanction of things as they are. But the judgment of God is upon the church as never before. If the church of today does not recapture the sacrificial spirit of the early church, it will lose its authentic ring, forfeit the loyalty of millions, and be dismissed as an irrelevant social club with no meaning for the 20th century. —Martin Luther King, Jr. *Letters From A Birmingham Jail*

~

Hugh Latimer, preaching at Cambridge in 1529, said, "I promise you if you build one hundred churches, give as much as you can to gilding of saints and honoring of the church; and if you go on as many pilgrimages as your body can withstand, and offer oaks as great candles; if you leave the works of mercy and the commandments undone, these works shall nothing avail you."

~

Jesus knew that "Love your enemies" didn't mean, "Don't make any."
-William Sloane Coffin

~

An exclusive men's club employed a Chinese cook. One afternoon, after an especially good lunch, the President called him into his office and said, "Mr. Kong, I'm going to give you a raise in salary." Mr. Kong inquired, "Why is that?" "Because you have been with us for eight years and you have done an excellent job for the club. We appreciate you and the work you've done," said the President. "Well, thank you, sir. But why did it take you eight years to notice?"

-Journal of Religious Speaking

~

Something akin to social dynamite is in this statement by the Roman Catholic Church from Vatican II:

God intended the earth and all it contains for the use of every human being and people. One should regard his lawful possessions not merely as his own, but also as common property in the sense that they should accrue to the benefit, not only to himself, but of others. The right to have a share of earthly goods sufficient for oneself and one's family belongs to everyone. If a person is in extreme necessity, he has the right to take from the riches of the others what he himself needs." That is not Karl Marx. Wonder if Congress has heard about that?

~

One Sunday afternoon in New York City a woman called the animal shelter to see if they could dispose of her dog which had died. They informed her they had no drivers on Sunday. She called the city's information number for sanitation services to ask if she could put her dog out with the garbage early in the morning. The official told her that was prohibited by law. Growing more frantic by the moment, she redialed the Animal Shelter and asked, "If I bring the dog to you today, will you dispose of it?" The manager said it was against regulations, but if she could deliver it, he would dispose of it. She placed the large dog in an old suitcase and began the long trip by subway to the animal shelter. She had to transfer trains twice. Reaching the Port Authority Building she was struggling to get on the escalator with the large suitcase, when a courteous young fellow said, "I've watched you carrying your suitcase. It must be very heavy. Can I carry it for you to your train?" The worn out woman was delighted. At last she could rest for a few minutes before she had to lug it one more time to the shelter. When they reached the top of the escalator, the young man ran and she never saw him again. That is justice.

~

If all were just there would be no need of valor. -Greek proverb

~

I think you know what I do to make a living,
but this is what I do to stay alive.

-Actor, Martin Sheen, speaking at the protest rally to close
the School of the Americas, Ft. Benning, GA, 11-20-04.

~

A table spread for the poor is an altar for the rich. —Rabbinic saying

~

Every few years there is some financial scandal in corporate America and every time thousands express doubts that the culprits will be brought to justice. One judge called the defendant to the bar for sentence. "Hancock Rutherford Allison Pritchet, IV, this court finds you guilty as charged on three counts of conspiracy to defraud the United States Government, twelve counts of mail fraud, and two counts of embezzling $6,000,000 dollars from the citizens of this state. I sentence you to six months in jail, suspended, and order you to pay a fine of $100,000. As a prominent citizen of this community, the ordeal and publicity of this case has caused you to suffer enough. Now, sir, please step forward for the ceremonial tapping of the wrists."

~

Upon accepting an award, the late Jack Benny said, "I really don't deserve this award, but I have arthritis and I don't deserve that either."

~

The churches have to feed the hungry, clothe the naked, and shelter the homeless. But they have also to remember that the answer to homelessness is homes, not shelters. What the poor and downtrodden need is not piecemeal charity, but wholesale justice. –William Sloane Coffin

~

A man said, "Sometime I'd like to ask God why God allows poverty, famine and injustice when something could be done about them." A friend replied, "Well, why don't you?" The reply: "Because I'm afraid God will ask me the same question."

~

Justice is not only blind; it has a hearing problem too. -Howard Kirksey

~

It is right for us to reach into the river of despair and rescue those who are drowning. But it is time for us to move upstream and discover who is throwing them in. -Bishop Edmund Browning

~

A young doctor's office was right beside a fast flowing river. One day she heard screaming and looked out the window to find a middle aged woman being swept away in the water. She and a few others managed to pull the woman to shore, but it was too late. She drowned. Shortly thereafter, another person was in trouble. Grabbing a rope, she was able to pull the man to safety. She cared for his wounds and put him in the hospital. In an hour another person was in trouble. After he was rescued, she closed her office and went upstream to discover why so many people found themselves in danger. She found a loose plank on the bridge that, when stepped on, gave way and dumped people into the water. When the plank on the bridge was repaired no more people were swept away. It is a noble work to care for the injured, but the most loving work the doctor did all day was to find the root cause of a social problem and fix it.

~

KNOWLEDGE

An astronomer sat next to a Christian theologian on a coast to coast flight. After pleasantries, he said, "I've done some reading in the Bible and theology and I've come to the conclusion that your field of work can all be summed up in "Jesus Loves Me This I Know For the Bible Tells Me So." The theologian replied, "That's an interesting observation. I've also done some reading in astronomy and I've come to the conclusion that astronomy can be summed up in "Twinkle, Twinkle Little Star."

~

The true value of knowledge is that it makes our ignorance more precise.
    -From Fugitive Pieces

~

A young child came home from her third grade class and asked her mother, "Momma, do I know now as much as I don't know?"

~

I do not pretend to know what many ignorant folks are sure of.   -Clarence Darrow

~

A little girl went over to her Grampa's house and exclaimed, "I've finished learning all the multiplication tables. Isn't that great!" Grampa told her how proud he was of her. "That calls for a celebration. Let's go get some ice cream!" While licking their cones, Grampa casually asked her with a twinkle in his eye, "I wonder what's 13 times 13?"

~

Ignorance is not bliss. It is oblivion.   --Philip Wylie

~

I wonder if we can really understand the world and the universe? It's tough enough reading most maps.
    —Unknown

~

I've tried to know absolutely nothing about a great many things and have succeeded fairly well.
    -Robert Benchley

~

Our knowledge is a receding mirage in an expanding desert of ignorance.
    -Will Durant

~

What man knows is everywhere at war with what he wants. -Joseph Krutch

~

A young minister was asked to speak to a children's Sunday school class on very short notice. "Well, children, what shall we talk about?" From the rear came a small voice, "What do you know?"

~

Knowledge fills a large brain. It inflates a small one. -Sydney Harris

~

We know nothing important. In the essentials we are still as wholly a mystery to ourselves as Adam was to himself.   -Booth Tarkington

~

Our knowledge grows in spots. The spots may be large or small, but the knowledge never grows all over; some old knowledge always remains what it was...Our minds grow in spots; and like grease-spots, the spots spread. But we let them spread as little as possible: we keep unaltered as much of our old knowledge and as many of our old prejudices and beliefs as we can. We patch and tinker more than we renew.   --William James, *Pragmatism*

~

To be conscious you are ignorant is a great step to knowledge. -Benjamin Disraeli

~

In the United States, there is a firmly established custom of sending researchers around the country to prove to ourselves how dumb we are.   -Calvin Trillin

~

Everybody is ignorant; only on different subjects. -Will Rogers

~

It ain't the things you don't know what gets you into trouble; it's the things you know for sure what ain't so. -Negro proverb. (Will Rogers is usually credited with this one.)

~

"Knowledge of God is not seen as an effort of the mind, but rather as an effect upon the mind. It is not to know so as to see the fact of God, but to know so as to feel the force of God in one's life. It is not knowledge as an acquisition, but knowledge as an impression."   -George Adam Smith

~

We're drowning in information and starving for knowledge. - Rutherford Rogers

~

Finagle's New Laws of Information
a. The information we have is not what we want.
b. The information we want is not what we need.
c. The information we need is not available.   --John Peers

~

I was recently on a tour of Latin America and the only regret I have was that I didn't study Latin harder in school so I could converse with those people.
-Vice President, Dan Quayle

~

There is no underestimating the intelligence of the American people.
-H. L. Mencken

~

I'm not young enough to know everything. –James Matthew Barrie

~

All of us want knowledge but few of us are willing to pay the price.

~

They say that knowledge is power. I used to think so, but I now know that they mean money.
–Lord Byron

~

As we know there are known knowns. There are things we know we know. We also know there are known unknowns. That is to say we know there are some things we do not know. But there are also unknown unknowns, the ones we don't know we don't know.
–Donald Rumsfeld, US Secretary of Defense at DOD Briefing, 2/12/2002

~

Professor Morris Bishop of Cornell University has written verse that pictures with sharp irony the flimsy foundation for life that we seem willing to construct as we trust science to be our ultimate hope.

> *What was our trust, we trust not;*
> *What was our faith, we doubt;*
> *Whether we must or must not,*
> *We may debate about;*
> *The soul perhaps is a gust of gas,*
> *And wrong is a form of right.*
> *But we know that energy equals mass,*
> *By the square of the speed of light.*
> *What we had known, we know not;*
> *What we have proved, abjure;*
> *Life is a tangled bowknot, but one thing still is sure:*
> *Come little lad, come little lass,*
> *Your docile creed recite:*
> *"We know that energy equals mass,*
> *By the square of the speed of light."*

~

Far more crucial than what we know or don't know is what we don't want to know.
-Eric Hoffer

~

As we struggle with our faith we may be encouraged by that old allegory which pictures knowledge as a strong, handsome knight, making his way across the great table land of the earth. With each step he tests the ground beneath his feet. Beside him and just above the ground moves the white-winged angel, Faith. Side by side they travel until they come to a steep cliff. Here the path suddenly stops and knowledge can go no further. It cannot test the ground beneath its feet. Only the leap of Faith can bridge the chasm, and knowledge is left behind.
–Unknown

~

> I keep six honest serving men
> (They taught me all I knew);
> Their names are What and Why and When
> And How and Where and Who.   -Rudyard Kipling

~

Half of knowledge is knowing where to find it. -On the entrance to the FSU Library.

LISTENING

The Lord gave us two ears and only one mouth. It's obvious. God expects us to listen twice as much as we speak.   -W.T. Martin, Jr.

~

Some people would rather be wrong than quiet.   −Unknown

~

There was an old owl lived in an oak
The more he heard, the less he spoke;
The less he spoke, the more he heard
O, if men were all like that wise bird.
--"Punch"

~

I learned to listen at my first dance. Nervous as a cat, I was dancing with the love of my life, going back and forth, and back and forth, wanting so much to get it right. I was concentrating so much on my dance step that Martha finally said, "Jimmy, the music's stopped."

~

An after-dinner speaker is like a corpse at a wake. He's necessary for the occasion, but you don't really expect to hear much from him.   -Dr. Garner Taylor

~

It makes a terrible death to be talked to death. -Mark Twain

~

The real value of freedom is not to the minority that wants to talk, but to the majority, that does not want to listen.   −Zechariah Chafee, Jr., American Educator

~

The old baseball veteran was a good hitter, but it was difficult for him to grasp life's subtleties. He got five hits in five times at bat on Saturday. However, Sunday's papers showed him four for five. He stormed into the official scorer's room and fumed, "I got five hits. Not four." The official scorer said, "I know. I know. It was a typographical error." "Error?" he thundered. "What do you mean, error? Nobody came within ten feet of any ball I hit all day."

~

The average woman talks fifty percent more than her husband listens. -J. Peer

~

An elderly woman was gently admonished for not wearing her hearing aid. She replied, "Actually dear, I've heard enough. I don't want to listen any more."

~

"If I had kept my mouth shut, I wouldn't be here," said the fish on the wall.

~

God gave us mouths that close and ears that don't. That should tell us something!

~

When you are answering your e mail and talking to your child, your cell phone is bound to ring. This is what Linda Stone of Microsoft calls *the state of continuous partial attention.*

~

Good umpires don't call plays at first base by sight. They call them as they hear them. Umps are taught to watch the base and see that the fielder has his foot on the bag. Then they hear the throw hit the glove. That way they can tell whether the runner or the ball gets there first. Fans might sing "Three blind mice" to the umps, but they never accuse them of being deaf.

~

There are none so deaf as those who will not hear. -Matthew Henry

~

Ruth Hettcamp, a German missionary friend in Tokyo, worked with young women who had moved to the city from the country. She provided a loving and secure environment and devoted her life to helping them adjust to city life. One of the residents, however, was a troublemaker. Ruth was patient and spoke frequently with her using her excellent Japanese to try and persuade her to develop a better attitude. Nevertheless, her unacceptable behavior continued. Finally, she could stand it no longer and called the young woman to her office. She motioned for her to sit down. When she did, she looked her in the eyes and spoke to her with the great emotion of her own native German language and said all of the things she kept bottled up inside. The young woman didn't understand a single word she said, but she listened to her and she changed!

~

His thoughts were slow,
His words were few
and never formed to glisten.
But he was a joy to all his friends,
You should have heard him listen.
-Unknown

~

Some people don't have much to say but you have to listen a long time to learn that.

-Unknown

~

A man was bragging to his friend about how good his new hearing aid was. His friend inquired, "What kind is it?" He replied, "Seven-thirty."

~

If you want someone to really listen to what you are saying, whisper.

~

Two senior citizens were finishing up their golf match on the eighteenth hole. One asked, "Is this Wednesday"? The other said, "No, it's Thursday." His friend replied, "Me too. Let's go get a beer."

~

LOVE

Jules Feiffer's cartoon speaks volumes. It portrays a man who announces, "I live inside a shell...That is inside a wall...That is inside a fort...That is inside a tunnel ...That is under the sea...Where I am safe...From you... If you really loved me, you'd find me."

~

You can't buy love. But it can cost you a bundle.

~

I'll believe in love when girls of twenty with money marry male paupers who have turned sixty.   -Elbert Hubbard, The Roycroft Dictionary and Book of Epigrams, 1923

~

The father recently died. There was great adjustment in the home as the family learned a new lifestyle. The son approached his mother washing the supper dishes and said, "Mom, I love you." The mother was touched. She dried her hands on a towel and then warmly hugged her son and said, "Jerry, I love you, too; but you know what I really need? I need you to show your love for me by picking up your clothes and taking out the trash." Love is a verb.

~

If love is the answer, could you rephrase the question. −Lily Tomlin

~

In a college course in public relations, the professor gave a pop quiz. Almost everyone answered all the questions except the last one. "What is the name of the cleaning lady in your dormitory?" The students wondered if this were a joke. One asked if the answer would count toward their grades. "Of course," replied the professor. "You're in public relations. Everybody you meet is significant. Everyone you meet is entitled to your attention and care."

~

About midnight, an older African American woman was standing beside her broken down car on the side of an Alabama highway in a thunderstorm. Soaking wet, she tried to flag down a ride. A young white man stopped to help her, generally unheard of in those conflict-filled 1960s. The man took her to safety, helped her get assistance, and put her into a taxicab. She seemed to be in a big hurry, but wrote down his address and thanked him. Seven days went by and a knock came on the man's door. To his surprise, a giant console color TV was delivered to his home. A special note was attached: "Thank you so much for assisting me on the highway the other night. The rain drenched not only my clothes, but also my spirits. Then you came along. Because of you, I was able to make it to my husband's bedside just before he passed away... God bless you for helping me and unselfishly serving others." Sincerely, Mrs. Nat King Cole

~

A deaf husband and a blind wife are always a happy couple. −Danish proverb

~

> Don't you know that it's a fool
> Who plays it cool
> By making his world a little colder.
> -Philip Slater, The Pursuit of Loneliness

~

Madelyn Murray O'Hare, a renowned atheist who had sued the government countless times for prayer in schools and public religious expressions, etc., said, "I've never met a Christian who didn't hate me."

~

Linus was sitting in the snow, shivering. Lucy walked by and ever so sweetly intoned, "Linus, be ye warmed and filled." And kept right on going.

--Charles M. Shulz,"Peanuts"

~

My wife invited some of the children in the church to have dinner in our home. One of the little boys, new to the group, followed her to the kitchen. As she was cleaning up he said, "I think I love you. But I'm not sure. I don't know you very well yet."

~

Lucy and Charlie Brown are having a conversation:
    Lucy: Our television screen is bigger than yours.
    Charlie Brown: "It is? That's nice. I'll bet you enjoy it!
    Lucy: My Dad makes more money than your Dad. And our house is a lot better than your house!
    Charlie Brown: I realize that and I'm very happy for you!
    Lucy: You drive me crazy!

-Charles M. Shulz, Peanuts

~

Lucy was talking to Patti: "People should be more kind to each other. Everyone should try and be gentle, considerate." "That's true!" replied Patti. Just then Charlie Brown shows up: Lucy yells from her depths, "Get out of here. Can't you see we are talking about love?"

-Charles M. Shulz, "Peanuts"

~

I was taught when I was young that if people would only love one another, all would be well with the world. This seemed simple and very nice; but I found when I tried to put it in practice not only that other people were seldom lovable, but that I was not very lovable myself.

–Geo. Bernard Shaw, Saint Joan

~

It was their first date and as they said good night at the door, the young woman looked deep into his eyes and said, "I've had a lovely evening, Raymond, and I must say, you were as warm and caring, witty and wise, and as enjoyable as your ad indicated you would be."

~

When you love someone you don't have to be continually talking.

~

The greatest love is a mother's, then a dog's, then a sweetheart's. -Polish proverb

~

The emotion of love, in spite of the romantics, is not self-sustaining; it endures only when the lovers love many things together, and not merely each other.

-Walter Lippmann

~

Patti is showing her class pictures to Charlie Brown. "There's Phil, the boy I told you about who loves me. And that's Sammy, who loves me, and Fred, who loves me, and William who loves me, and..." Charlie inquired, "All those boys love you?" Patti responds, "When no one loves you, you have to pretend that everyone loves you!"

-Charles M. Shulz, "Peanuts"

~

Keith Davis in a 1985 issue of "Psychology Today" wrote an article comparing love and friendship. It contains several quotes that are worthwhile: Dave Tyson Gentry: "True friendship comes when silence between two people is comfortable."

~

John Ciardi: "Love is the word used to label the sexual excitement of the young, the habituation of the middle-aged, and the mutual dependence of the old." And Franklin P. Jones says, "Love doesn't make the world go round. Love makes the ride worthwhile."

-"Context"

~

Sometimes love says what needs to be said. In the comic strip, "Peanuts", Patti has seen a recent picture of Santa Claus and is very upset. She dashes off a quick letter: "Dear Santa, I saw a picture of you in the paper today. You sure are getting fat. You look like you just ate all your reindeer. You're going to be sorry next summer when you can't get into your swim trunks. Get out of Scarf City before it's too late. I am enclosing a special diet for you. Stick to it!" Then she says to Charlie Brown, "He'll probably hate me, but it is for his own good." And Charlie Brown, just a few days before Christmas, replies, "The rest of us who also love him, thank you!"

-Charles M. Shulz, "Peanuts"

~

Love is silence when your words would hurt.
Love is patience when your neighbor's curt.
Love is deafness when the scandal flows.
Love is thoughtfulness for another's woes.
Love is promptness when stern duty calls.
Love is courage when misfortune falls.

--Unknown

~

Love does not consist in gazing at each other but in looking outward together in the same direction.

—Antoine de Saint- Exupery

~

A nervous fellow cautiously asked a young woman in his office, "Do you think you could ever learn to love a person like me?" She hesitated a moment and then asked, "How much like you?"

~

You can give without loving. But you cannot love without giving. -James Hewett

~

"Father," asked the young man, "what is charity?" The old man laid down the paper and said, "Charity, my boy is giving away something you don't want."
"Well, Dad, what is organized charity?" That took a little more explanation: "Organized charity, Son, is giving away something you don't want to somebody who doesn't want it, who will give it to somebody else who will lose it." The young fellow said, "I understand, Father, but what is love?" The father replied, "Well now, what is love? Why, love is sharing something you would like to keep with somebody who needs it more than you do, but I want you to know, son, that love is mighty expensive. It costs a heap!" -Unknown

~

My Grandson walked with me from the hotel to the shuttle bus for the airport. As a bus pulled up to the curb, he planted a big kiss on my cheek. But, upon learning that the bus was going elsewhere, he said matter of factly, "I kissed you all for nothing didn't I?" Actually, I didn't mind.

~

If you have no love in your heart, you have the worst kind of heart trouble. -Bob Hope

~

There are 58 million dogs in the US; 28 million dog owners buy them Christmas gifts every year. Nearly 10 million celebrate their dog's birthdays; 17% say they keep a picture of their pet in their purse or wallet. More than 6 million say they are as attached to their dogs as they are to their children. -"Governing Magazine"

~

We are shaped and fashioned by what we love. –Johann Wolfgang von Goethe

~

A soldier said to a buddy as he left the base, "This has got to be love at first sight. I've only got an eight-hour pass."

~

The way to love anything is to realize that it might be lost. –G.K. Chesterton

~

I never knew how to worship until I knew how to love. –Henry Ward Beecher

~

The kiss was "invented" in India, but it was the Romans who popularized it around the world. An equal kissed another on the lips. The lower one on the socio-economic scale kissed another on the cheek, arm, hand, or feet. In early New England the Puritans sought to banish the kiss from society.

~

Charity begins at home, and mostly ends where it begins. –Horace Smith

~

When I walk on the beach to watch a sunset I do not call out, "A little more orange over to the right please," or "Would you mind giving us less purple in the back?" No, I enjoy the always-different sunsets as they are. We do well to do the same with people we love. –Carl Rogers

~

MIRACLE

Shortly after each of my grandchildren were born, my son and daughter held the phone nearby so I could hear them gurgle or cry. They were *eloquent*! No other word will do. Their little voices silenced all the arguments of the cynics who say that there is no God.   -Psalm 8

~

Miracles happen to those who believe in them. —Bernard Berenson

~

A man was ridiculed by his drinking buddies when he became a Christian. "What about this Jesus? ...You don't believe all that stuff about Him, do you? ... turning water into wine and all that business?" He replied, "I'm not sure about a lot of it myself, but what I do know is God has changed beer into furniture in my house. And that's miracle enough for me!"

~

Today's greatest miracle is how the church works so hard to turn the marvelous tasty wine of the Gospel into water.

~

A minister ended his children's message with an exhortation for them to kneel down beside their beds tonight and pray. One little fellow said, "If I do, it will be a miracle. I sleep on the top bunk."

~

We don't believe in miracles. We rely on them. —Unknown

~

All of us are uneasy in the presence of a miracle. St. Peter and St. Thomas were playing golf on one of the heavenly courses. St. Thomas teed off and the ball went straight for the pin and dropped. A hole in one. St. Peter said, "Great shot, Thomas!" Then he teed off. Again, the ball went straight for the pin and dropped. Another hole in one. "Good shot, Peter," said St. Thomas. "Now, why don't we quit the miracles and play golf?"

~

Some people cast their bread on the waters and expect it to return as French toast.
                                                                                      -Unknown

~

Whatever a man prays for, he prays for a miracle. Every prayer reduces itself to this: Great God, grant that twice two be not four.   -Ivan Turgenev

~

One miracle is just as easy to believe as another. -William Jennings Bryan

~

When we see ourselves on the edge of an abyss and it seems that God has abandoned us, we no longer hesitate to expect a miracle.   -William Prynne

~

65

Miracle is simply the wonder of the unique that points us back to the wonder of the everyday.

—Maurice Friedman

~

We find a miracle only when we stop looking for magic. -Ernest Kurtz

~

When the French Revolutionist, Comte de Mirabeau was told something was impossible, he replied, "Never mention to me again that blockhead of a word."

~

The Sunday school teacher was carefully explaining the story of Elijah the prophet and the false prophets of Baal. She explained how Elijah built the altar, put wood upon it, cut the steer in pieces, and laid it upon the altar. And then she told them how Elijah commanded the people to fill four barrels of water and pour it over the altar four times. "Now, can anyone in the class tell me why the Lord would have Elijah pour water over the steer on the altar?" A little girl in the back of the room started waving her hand, "I know! I know!" she said, "To make the gravy!"

~

A group of high school students were studying the Seven Wonders of the World. At the end of the session they were asked to list today's Seven Wonders of the World. There was disagreement, but the following got the most votes:

Egypt's Great Pyramids, Taj Mahal, Grand Canyon, Panama Canal,
Empire State Building, St. Peter's Basilica and China's Great Wall.

While gathering the votes, the teacher recognized that one student hadn't turned in her paper yet. She asked if she were having trouble with the list. "Yes, a little. I couldn't quite make up my mind because there are so many." The teacher said, "Tell us what you have and maybe we can help." The girl hesitated, then read, "I think the seven wonders of the world are:

To touch, to taste, to see, to hear, to feel, to laugh, and to love."

The silence was deafening. It is far too easy for us to look at the exploits of human beings and refer to them as wonders, and overlook the wonders God has wrought.

-Unknown

~

A Sunday school teacher asked her class what they considered the greatest miracle in the Bible. One little boy answered, "When God told his Son to stand still and he obeyed."

~

A Scotsman, on a trip to the Holy Land, was aghast when he was told it would cost fifty dollars an hour to rent a boat on the Sea of Galilee. "Hoot, mon!" he said, "In Scotland it would'na hae been more than $20!" That might be true," said the agent, "but you have to take into account that the Sea of Galilee is water on which our Lord himself walked."
"Well, at $50 an hour for a boat," said the Scotsman, "it's no wonder he walked!"

~

One of the priests at the Sanctuario de Chimayo, NM, sometimes called "The Lourdes of America", had a conversation with an NPR reporter about the Sanctuario where dozens of crutches line a wall, discarded by those who claimed a miracle healing and thousands of visitors cart away "holy dirt" to use in other places, believing it has healing properties. The reporter asked the priest if the legend was true that God replenished the dirt. "No," replied the priest, "God's far too busy for that. We order 25 tons of fresh dirt each year."

~

When Charles Lindbergh landed in France after his trans-Atlantic flight, the news was broadcast all over the world. A secretary, hearing of this miracle, burst into the office of her boss exclaiming, "Mr. Murphy, Mr. Murphy, a man has just flown from New York to Paris all by himself." The boss continued to work and showed no interest. She cried out again, "Don't you understand? A mans has just flown all the way across the Atlantic Ocean, by himself." Murphy said, "All by himself? A man can do anything! When a committee flies the Atlantic, call me."

-"Journal of Religious Speaking"

~

Bill was bragging to his friends about his new golden retriever. "He's the best dog I've ever seen. He's a miracle dog. And if you don't believe he's a miracle dog, I'll prove it to you if you come to my duck blind next Saturday morning." Two of his friends took him up on it. They were all crouched down in the blind when Bill said, "Everybody still, now. Here come the ducks." He knocked one down with his shotgun and said, "Go get 'em, Goldie." So Goldie leaped out of the blind and walked right up on the water to the place where the duck was. He picked it up and brought it back to his master. "See anything different about that doc?" Bill asked his friends. "Yeah, one said, "He can't swim."

~

When asked what the most appealing miracle Jesus performed was, a young fellow replied, the one where everybody loafed and fished.

~

MYSTERY

The chicken probably came before the egg. It is hard to imagine God sitting on an egg.
-Anonymous

~

The American people have had their sense of mystery and awe bred right out of them, just like chickens who have had their wings bred right off of them.
--Flannery O'Connor

~

One of life's ultimate mysteries is how that son or daughter-in-law whom you knew was not good enough for your child became the parent of the world's smartest grandchild.

~

It is not hard to know God, provided one will not force oneself to define Him.
−Unknown

~

With all of our accumulated wisdom, people have submitted rewrites to Twinkle, twinkle, little star. The winner is:

Twinkle, twinkle, little star,
Now I know just what you are
An incandescent ball of gas
Surrounded by a swirling mass.

~

The popular actor, Danny Thomas, told of a young boy who was being questioned for Confirmation by his Bishop. "My boy," said the Bishop, "what is the Trinity?" The young fellow had a speech defect, but nevertheless answered, "Father, Son, and Holy Spirit." The Bishop leaned closer, "I couldn't understand." The bright youngster responded, "You're not supposed to understand, it's a mystery."
-David MacLennan, Church Chuckles

~

Concepts create idols; only wonder comprehends anything. People kill one another over idols. Wonder makes us fall to our knees.
-Saint Gregory

~

After they had a lesson on Jacob in the Old Testament, a Catholic Priest visited the classroom and asked the children if they had any questions he might be able to answer. One little girl asked, "If the angels had wings, why did they walk up and down on Jacob's ladder?" The man of God replied, "Would any of you children like to answer that question?"
−Msgr. Arthur Tonne, Jokes Priests Can Tell

~

A chicken and an egg are lying in bed. The chicken is smoking a cigarette with a smile on his face. The egg is frowning with disappointment. The egg mutters under his breath, "Well, I guess we answered THAT question."

~

When we remember we are all mad, the mysteries disappear and life stands explained.   —Mark Twain

~

The problem of evil has baffled mankind since Eden; perhaps because it can only be approached through facing the mystery of what is good, and we do not like to acknowledge that good is a mystery.   -D. M. Dooling

~

Every time the sacred text describes a fact, it reveals a mystery. —St. Gregory

~

People travel to wonder at the height of mountains, at the huge waves of the sea, at the long courses of rivers, at the vast compass of the ocean, at the circular motion of the stars; and they pass by themselves without wondering.
                                              -St. Augustine, 354-430 A.D.

~

We all know the expression, "the bread always falls on its buttered side." One day the bread fell buttered side up. A man scooped up the piece of bread and ran to his rabbi's office to report on a fundamental change in the rules of the universe. The Rabbi was dumbfounded and said it was beyond his level of competence. He referred him to the Talmudic School of London. They debated the problem for weeks before they came upon the solution... The bread was obviously buttered on the wrong side.

~

Flannery O'Connor said, "Mystery is the great embarrassment to the modern mind. The task of the novelist is to deepen mystery."

~

God in His wisdom made the fly and then forgot to tell us why. —Ogden Nash

~

The world is sure crazy, when the best rapper is a white man and the best golfer is a black man; when the tallest player in the NBA is Chinese; and the French are criticizing the Americans for being arrogant and the Germans don't want to go to war.   —Charles Barclay, professional basketball player, 2003

~

Benjamin Constant tells of a Piedmont peasant who thought the world was made by a God who died before his work was completed.

~

After 40 years of farming he retired and took his wife to London. Their guide took them into the majestic sanctuary of St Paul's Church. Under that magnificent dome he looked up in awe and said, "Just think how much silage you could put in a place like this."

~

The most beautiful and most profound emotion we can experience is the sensation of the mystical. It is the power of all true science. He to whom this emotion is a stranger, who can no longer wonder and stand rapt in awe, is as good as dead.   -Albert Einstein

~

In Martin Marty's book, *The Fire We Can Light*, he laments that the sense of wonder is disappearing from the minds of the young and the gifted. He tells of William Hamilton and his son who were looking up into the sky full of stars that gave Pascal and Kant and millions of others a sense of awe and mystery. The boy asked, "Dad, which ones did we put up there?"

~

In the novel, *The Magus*, by John Fowles, the young man, Nicholas says, "I didn't know where I was going, but I knew what I needed. I needed a new love, a new race, a new language; and although I couldn't have put it into words then, I needed a new mystery."

~

At the close of a day, a father and mother with their children were watching a beautiful sunset and everybody was quiet. No one broke the silence until the three year old boy took his father's hand and said, "Daddy, I think we ought to say the blessing."

~

Samuel M. Carothers tells of a young man who left with him a manuscript for criticism, and remarked in passing, "it is only a little bit of my work, and it will not take you long to look it over. In fact, it is only the first chapter in which I explain the Universe."   -Quoted by Harry Emerson Fosdick, *The Meaning of Faith*

~

The truth is men have lost their belief in the Invisible. It is no longer a worship of the Beautiful and Good, but a calculation of the profitable.   –Thomas Carlyle

~

The philosopher aspires to explain away all mysteries, to dissolve them into light. Mystery, on the other hand, is demanded and pursued by the religious instinct; mystery constitutes the essence of worship.   –Henri Amiel, philosopher

~

A farmer who needed to sell some steers at the stock market in Louisville, Kentucky, invited a neighbor to accompany him on the 60 mile trip. His guest had never been beyond the county line before. On the way up to the market he talked incessantly. But on the way back, he was stone silent. As they came back to familiar territory, he suddenly exclaimed, "John, let me tell you something. If there's as much land on the other side of Louisville as there is between here and Louisville, this is a big world!"   --Ben Fisher, *Mountain Preacher Stories*

~

One of the greatest mysteries in the world is what a nudist does with the keys once he locks his car.   –J.M. Braude

~

PATIENCE*

"QUICK! GIVE ME PATIENCE!"

A handful of patience is worth more than a bushel of brains.   -Dutch proverb

~

A brusque businessman prayed that God would give him patience. Shortly thereafter a new secretary was hired and she was very slow. He confided to his friend, "This secretary I've just hired is driving me crazy. I've asked God to give me patience, but I can't seem to get it." The friend, asked, "Did you ever think your secretary may be God's answer to your prayer?"

~

Patience is bitter but its fruit is sweet. -French proverb

~

Peace Corps volunteers in Brazil were given these instructions in the event of an attack by a hungry python: "Remember not to run away, the python can move faster. The thing to do is lie flat on the ground on your back with your feet together, arms at your side, head well down. The python will try to push its head under you, experimenting at every possible point. Keep calm. You must let him swallow your foot. It is quite painless and will take a long time. If you lose your head and struggle, he will quickly whip his coils around you. If you keep calm and still he will go on swallowing. Wait patiently until he has swallowed up to about your knee. Then carefully take out your knife and insert it into the distended side of his mouth and with a quick rip slit him up."
                                                    -Hoover Rupert, "Presbyterian Outlook"

~

I'm extraordinarily patient, provided I get my own way in the end.
                        —Margaret Thatcher

~

* See also WAITING

71

He was a bona fide couch potato and the wife was running out of patience. She says, "It's no use, Gerald. We tried counseling; we tried Prozac; and you're still hopeless."

~

As a teenager I always listened to the "Saturday Game of the Day" with Dizzy Dean and Pee Wee Reese. I was intrigued by Pee Wee's public service announcement, "Remember, if you're drowning, keep calm."

~

Don Asse (pronounced ah'see) was a relief pitcher for the California Angels and Baltimore Orioles. He had one recurring dream throughout his life: a line drive was ready to hit him square in the face. He would flail his arms and get them in front of his face and scream. When he got married, his wife, Judy, for the first months and years was almost shell-shocked. But after a few years, she would wake up in the middle of the night to this horrible scream and simply say, "Line drive, huh, Don?"

~

A woman spent hours doing the family wash; but when she hung up the last piece of clothes, the sagging line snapped. All the clean clothes fell to the ground. Without a word she gathered them in her arms and washed them again. This time she spread them out to dry on the grassy area of her back yard. Then a big neighborhood dog came running through the yard and left his tracks on the twice cleaned clothes. As she gathered them once again in her arms a little smile came across her face. Said she, "Now, ain't that funny. He didn't miss a one."   - Unknown

~

Patience has its limits. Taken too far, its cowardice. -George Jackson

~

If there were no other proof of the infinite patience of Christ in His dealings with us, a very good proof could be found in His toleration of the pictures that are painted of Him and of the noise that proceeds from musical instruments under the pretext of being in His honor."   -Thomas Merton, *The Commonweal Reader*

~

Wanting to make a left turn onto a busy highway, I was annoyed by the extreme caution of the driver in front of me, but, grateful for the patience of the driver in back of me when it was my turn to venture out on the highway and make the turn.

~

The lovely thing about patience is that it annoys the person who is annoying you.
          -Howard Kirksey

~

Parking places aren't all that hard to find. Look how many people find them before you do.   -Unknown

~

There was one stage a week from New York to Philadelphia. If our forebears missed it, they'd sit patiently and wait a week for another one. Today our whole day is ruined if we miss one section of a revolving door.   -Dr. Howard Danforth

~

There was never yet a philosopher who could bear a toothache patiently.
-William Shakespeare

~

Patience: a minor form of despair disguised as virtue.   -Ambrose Bierce

~

If you are patient in a moment of anger, you will escape a hundred days of sorrow.
--Chinese proverb

~

Sitting in a boat in the middle of the lake, a disgruntled fisherman said to his partner, "Dog gone it, Bob. This is the second time in an hour that you have crossed and uncrossed your feet. Did you come out here to dance or to fish?"

~

Patience is putting up with people you'd like to put down. –Anonymous

~

If you want to make friends with a squirrel you can't run at it. -One child to another

~

GOD GIVE ME PATIENCE AND I NEED IT RIGHT NOW.

~

Beware the fury of a patient man. –John Dryden

~

In Sumatra, a woman lived with her husband and two children in a tiny grass hut. When her in-law's house was blown away in a typhoon they were invited to move in. The crowded hut got on her nerves. In desperation she went to the wisest shaman in the village. "What am I going to do?" she begged. He counseled her to bring her two pigs into the hut and come back and see him next week. She returned saying, "I can't go on like this." "Oh, yes, you can. Trust me!" said the shaman. "Now put your ducks and rabbits in the house too and if you have any chickens put them in the hut, and come back and see me next week." "I don't believe you understand my situation," she said, "but, I'll do what you say." A week later she was back. "I'm completely out of control. I can't even move in my own house. There are people and animals everywhere." "All right," said the wise man, "take out the ducks and rabbits and come see me next week." The next week she said, "With the ducks and the rabbits gone, things were better, but she was still miserable." "All right," said the wise man, "Take out the pigs. That will solve your problem." And it did.   -Journal of Religious Speaking

~

The genius of patience: doing something else in the meantime.

~

PEACE

In the wake of the defeat of the Ottoman Empire on the Eastern Front in World War I, Winston Churchill redrew the map of the Middle East, without regard to the history, the demographics, and the cultures of the region, creating new nation states with artificial boundaries. Field Marshall Archibald Wavell remarked, "We have just fought a war to end all wars; now they are signing a peace to end all peace."

~

Washington, DC, is full of monuments to peace. We build one after every war.
--Unknown

~

A peace loving nation is one that outlaws firecrackers and makes hydrogen bombs.

~

The mystery of peace is located in the nature and quality of relationship developed with those most feared. -John Paul Lederach, *The Moral Imagination*

~

A University of California study reveals that the person most likely to be working for humanitarian causes and world peace today isn't the young college student. It's your grandmother. The most politically active people in the United States today are grandmothers. -"Context"

~

In 1919, President Woodrow Wilson met with the president of France, and the prime minister of England. The president of France asked, "Do we really want peace?" They replied, "Yes." "Well then, England will give up India, the US will give up the dollar rights to Cuba, Latin America and the Philippines, and France will give up Southeast Asia and Africa." Wilson and the English prime minister said, "You don't understand what we mean by peace." The president of France responded, "You don't want peace, you want quietness." -George Thomas Tate

If they want peace, nations should avoid the pin-pricks that precede cannon-shots.
–Napoleon Bonaparte

~

Peace, n. In international affairs, a period of cheating between two periods of fighting. -Ambrose Bierce

~

That which comes into the world to disturb nothing deserves neither respect nor patience. –Rene Char

~

I do not believe that any peacock envies another peacock his tail, because every peacock is persuaded that his own tail is the finest in the world. The consequence of this is that peacocks are peaceful birds. –Bertrand Russell, 1872-1970

~

There is no way to peace along the way to safety. For peace must be dared. It is the great venture. —Dietrich Bonhoeffer, The Church and the Peoples of the World

~

Wars are bred by poverty and oppression. Continued peace is possible only in a relatively free and prosperous world. -George Marshall, American Secretary of State

~

I was leaving Memorial Stadium in Baltimore when in front of me some young men got into a vicious fight. One kicked another in the head as he lay on the ground. I grabbed him and held on, as I said to myself, "Now you've played the fool, Atwood, what are you going to do next?" The young fellow asked, "What are you doing?" I replied, "I saw you kick that guy in the head and I'm not going to let you do it any more." I knew I was in a difficult spot and wished for a policeman. When one miraculously appeared, I gratefully turned the matter over to him. But, I left the stadium with an existential understanding of how risky it is to try and bring peace to a violent situation.

~

I LOVE WAR. PEACE WILL BE HELL FOR ME. —General George Patton

~

Five great enemies to peace live within us: avarice, ambition, envy, anger, and pride. If those enemies were to be banished we should infallibly enjoy perfect peace. -Francesco Petrarch, Italian Poet, 1304-1374

~

With whom will we warring nations make peace? With our friends? With whom will we negotiate? With those who think exactly as we do? With whom will we make peace? With those who have treated us well or with those who have in the past harmed us? -Anonymous

~

Ramsey MacDonald, the former Prime Minister of England, was once working on a peace plan with an official of the government who was an expert in foreign affairs. He was cynical over the entire prospect and said, "The desire for peace does not necessarily ensure it." "That's true," replied MacDonald. "Neither does your appetite satisfy your hunger but it gets you moving toward a restaurant."

~

Russia has a dictator who dreams of peace and thinks he can reach it across a sea of blood. —Mohandas Gandhi

~

Modern war does not prove who is right. It proves who is left. —Unknown

~

A sure certainty about our Memorial Days is as fast as the ranks from one war thin out, the ranks from another take their place. Prominent men run out of Decoration Day Speeches, but the world never runs out of wars. People talk peace, but men give their life's work to war. I won't talk peace until there is as much brains and scientific study put to aid peace as there is to promote war. -Will Rogers

~

The Bible says, "The lion and the lamb shall lie down together."
Woody Allen adds, "But the lamb won't get much sleep."

~

What a beautiful fix we're in now. Peace has been declared.
-Napoleon, following peace agreement at Amiens

~

"Tell me the weight of a snowflake," a coal mouse asked a wild dove. "Nothing more than nothing," was the answer. "In that case I must tell you a marvelous story," the coal mouse said. "I sat on a fir branch, close to the trunk, when it began to snow. It was not a raging storm or blizzard. No, it was just like in a dream, without any violence. Since I didn't have anything better to do, I began to count the snowflakes settling on the twigs and needles of my branch. Their number reached exactly 3,471,952. When the next snowflake dropped gently onto the branch, weighing nothing more than nothing, the branch broke off and fell to the ground." Having said that, the coal mouse ran away. The dove, since Noah's time an authority on the matter, gave much thought concerning the story and said to herself, "Perhaps there is only one person's voice lacking for peace to come about in the world."

--Bulletin Board, Wesley Theological Seminary

~

No pacifists or Communists are going to govern this country. If they try it there will be seven million men like you rise up and strangle them. Pacifists? Hell, I'm a pacifist, but I always have a club behind my back.

-Smedley Butler, US Marine Commander

~

Mort Walker, in his comic strip, *Beetle Bailey*, has a point. The Sergeant is on the firing range watching Beetle shoot his rifle. Beetle suddenly turns philosophical..."Sarge, why do we have to do all this war training?" The Sarge replies, "Because in over 3,000 years of history there were less than 300 years of peace." Beetle asks another question, "Wouldn't it be more important then to train for more years of peace?"

~

I prefer the most unfair peace to the most righteous war. –Cicero

~

If the pursuit of peace is both old and new, it is also both complicated and simple. It is complicated, for it has to do with people, and nothing in this universe baffles man as much as man himself.   -Adlai Stevenson, 1952

~

It takes more courage to work for peace than it does to work for war. You can rally a group of people to fight against an enemy so much easier than you can rally a group of people to make peace with an enemy. So, in spite of a universal vision for peace, it takes more courage to break the circle of hatred and revenge than it does to perpetuate it.   –Unknown

~

When I pray for peace, I pray not only that the enemies of my own country may cease to want war, but also I pray that my own country will cease to do the things that make war inevitable.   –Thomas Merton

POVERTY

He was rich, yet for your sake he became poor, so that through his poverty you might become rich.
    –II Corinthians 8:9

~

Poverty is the open-mouthed relentless hell which yawns beneath civilized society, and it is hell enough.
    –Henry George

~

Nobody gets to heaven without a letter of reference from the poor. –James Forbes

~

I used to think I was poor. Then they told me I wasn't poor, I was needy. Then they told me it was self-defeating to think of myself as needy, I was deprived. Then they told me underprivileged was overused. I was disadvantaged. I still don't have a dime. But I have a great vocabulary.
    –Jules Feiffer

~

Remember the poor- it costs nothing. -Josh Billings

~

The Democrats declared war on poverty. Apparently poverty won.
    –Ronald Reagan

~

I wasn't born in a log cabin but my family moved into one as soon as they could afford it.
    -Malville D. Landon

~

A burglar entered the home of a social worker late at night. When the man stirred in his bed, the burglar put a knife to his throat and said, "I'm here looking only for money. I won't hurt you; but if you make any noise, you're a dead man." The man said, "I don't think you'll find any money in this house. But if you'll let me turn on the light, I'll help you look." The burglar left the house laughing.
    –Unknown

~

Poverty is no disgrace but it's very inconvenient. -Sydney Smith

~

Poverty breeds lack of self-reliance. --Daniel DeLeon

~

When money is an idol to be poor is a sin. --William Stringfellow

~

Undershaft, one of George Bernard Shaw's characters, says, "Poverty is the worst of crimes. All the other crimes are virtues beside it. All other dishonors are chivalry itself by comparison."

~

It is no disgrace to be poor but it might as well be. –Jim Grue

~

In 1967, Los Angeles, Detroit, New York, Newark and dozens of other large cities exploded into riot revealing the bitter, deep-rooted dissensions of 300 years of exploitation and injustice. In 1968, President Lyndon Johnson appointed a large commission to report on the roots of rising militancy in the country and the widening gap between black and white Americans. He said, "The only genuine, long range solution for what has happened lies in an attack mounted at every level upon the conditions that breed despair and violence. All of us know what those conditions are: ignorance, discrimination, slums, poverty, disease, not enough jobs. We should attack these conditions not because we are frightened by conflict, but because we are fired by conscience. We should attack them because there is simply no other way to achieve a decent and orderly society in America."

One of the first witnesses before the commission was Dr. Kenneth Clarke. Referring to the reports of earlier riot commissions, he said, "I read the report of the 1919 riot in Chicago and it is as if I were reading the investigating committee of the Harlem riots of 1935...and the report of the Harlem riot in 1943, and the Watts riot of 1965. It's a kind of Alice in Wonderland with the same moving picture, re-shown over and over again; the same analysis, the same recommendations, and the same inaction."

~

A little girl is holding tightly to her doll and crying. Her mother tries to calm her daughter's fears. "Good gracious, honey," she says. "Yes, daddy did say, 'We can't afford any more taxes without going into the poor house'." But that doesn't mean we don't have any money. Sweetheart, we've got lots of money."

~

It is ironic to think of the number of people in this country who pray for the poor and needy on Sunday and spend the rest of week complaining that the government is doing something about them.　　　　　—William Sloane Coffin

~

Poverty is expensive to maintain.　-Michael Harrington

~

Toyohiko Kagawa, after graduating from the Presbyterian Seminary in Kobe, Japan, was acutely aware of the Christian responsibility for the poor. He moved to the slums of Kobe and lived a marginal existence among the unemployed, the sick, and outcasts. When a teacher at the seminary heard of his tenuous health, he went to the slums and found him living in a hovel. He asked, "What are you doing here in these conditions?" Kagawa answered, "Sensei, (teacher) what are you doing living out there?"

~

No one can love his neighbor on an empty stomach.　—President Woodrow Wilson

~

Of all the preposterous assumptions of humanity, nothing exceeds most of the criticisms made on the habits of the poor by the well-housed, well-warmed, and well fed.　　　　　-Herman Melville

~

THE GREATEST MAN IN HISTORY WAS THE POOREST.
–Ralph Waldo Emerson

~

Eugene O'Neill once wrote, "The child was diseased at birth, stricken with a hereditary ill that only the most vital are able to shake off. I mean poverty—the most deadly and prevalent of all diseases."

~

Once on the Great Sabbath (before the Passover) the rabbi of Roptchitz came home from the house of prayer with weary steps. "What made you so tired?" asked his wife. "It was the sermon," he replied. "I had to speak of the poor and their many needs for the coming Passover. Unleavened bread and wine and everything else is terribly high this year." "And what did you accomplish with your sermon?" his wife asked. "Half of what is needed," he answered. "The poor are now ready to receive help. Whether the rich are ready to give—I don't know about that yet."   -William B. Silverman

~

A German missionary friend in Nepal committed herself to living as close to Nepalese living standards as she possibly could, yet found it very difficult. She not only had a much lower standard of living, but endured the comments of the children. Every afternoon the children would come to her window sill and prop their chins on their hands and say, "My, how rich you are; you have a picture on your wall. My, how rich you are; you have four potatoes for dinner. My, how rich you are; you have a day off." If the average bread earner took a day off in Nepal, the family wouldn't eat tomorrow.

~

If war no longer occupied men's thoughts and energies, we would, within a generation, put an end to all serious poverty throughout the world.
                                                  -Bertrand A. Russell

~

We shall soon, with the help of God, be in sight of the day when poverty will be banished from this nation.   —President Herbert Clark Hoover

~

In a country well governed poverty is something to be ashamed of. In a country badly governed wealth is something to be ashamed of.   —Confucius

~

I wish to become rich, so that I can instruct the people and glorify honest poverty a little, like those kind-hearted, fat, benevolent people do.   —Mark Twain

PREPARATION*

The little girl had a sixth sense. She watched her mother vacuum the living room and inquired, "Mommy, who's coming to visit?"

~

Jack was always thinking about how he could save a buck. He reasoned that it was going to snow only 25 percent of the time. So he went out and bought one snow tire.

~

A Scottish preacher had a family emergency and asked a neighboring colleague to conduct a graveside service for one of his members. The pastor agreed to help his friend. He was told the family wanted a very brief service with no remarks. This meant he would not need to spend time in preparation. He took his friend literally and made no plans other than to use the simple liturgy provided in The Book of Common Worship. Getting to the committal portion of the service, he suddenly realized he didn't know whether the deceased was a man or woman. The rubrics read, "Unto the mercy of Almighty God we commend the soul of our brother/sister departed and we commit his/her body to the ground, earth to earth, dust to dust, etc. He leaned over and whispered to the gentleman standing next to him, "Be the deceased brother or sister?" The man replied, "Neither, cousin."

~

The golfer teed off and lost his ball and proceeded to scold the caddy because he too didn't know where it went. "Why weren't you watching more closely?" he asked. Said the caddy, "Sir, it usually doesn't go anywhere and I was unprepared."

~

WANT TO MAKE GOD LAUGH? --- MAKE A PLAN

~

I met a young seminary student who took great delight in announcing he would not buy life insurance. "God is my life insurance policy. God will always look after me", he said. In one sense, he's perfectly right, but in another sense, what he calls God, I call mooching. Someone in his family or church must come to his aid in the event of a tragedy or death.

~

Forewarned, forearmed; prepared is half the victory.   -Spanish proverb

~

A wise rule is to make up your mind soberly what you want, peace or war, and then get ready for what you want; for what we prepare for is what we shall get.
-William Sumner

~

Luck is a matter of preparation meeting opportunity.   -Oprah Winfrey

~

* See SEEKING

A man and wife spent months planning their photography safari to Kenya. The second day out, a lion pounced on the husband and was ready to eat him alive. He shouted out, "Shoot, Marge, shoot! Marge, shoot!" Marge replied, "I can't dear, I'm out of film."

~

Plan ahead. It wasn't raining when Noah built the ark.   –Unknown

~

I wake up every morning determined to change the world and to have one hell of a good time. Sometimes this makes planning the day a little difficult.   --E. B. White

~

In human endeavor, chance favors the prepared mind. –Louis Pasteur

~

Careers, like rockets, don't always take off on schedule. The key is to keep working on the engines.   -Gary Sinise

~

The Bible Society had a sign in front of their building, "Prepare to meet the Author."

~

The Anglican priest always wrote down the names of those who were to be married in his prayer book on Post-it tabs. However the bride and groom for this wedding were very active in the Parish and he knew them well and determined that he would not need to jot down their names. When his mind went blank he was too embarrassed to ask their names so he devised what sounded like an authentic prayer book question: "In what names dost thou come to God's House?" The groom was taken back for a moment but replied in great dignity, "We come in the name of the Father, Son, and Holy Ghost."   –Ronald Brown

~

In a cemetery in Indiana is this epitaph:
Pause stranger, when you pass me by,
As you are now, so once was I.
As I am now, so you will be,
So prepare for death and follow me.
Someone who passed by scratched this reply:
To follow you I'm not content
Until I know which way you went.
-James S. Hewett

~

Winning can be defined as the science of being totally prepared.
–George Allen, football coach

~

PROVIDENCE

"Do You INSURE CHURCHES AGAINST
ACTS OF GOD?"

Golda Meir, former Prime Minister of Israel, wondered aloud about God's providence. "If God chose the People of Israel and led us through the desert, why did God lead us to the only place in the Middle East that didn't have oil?"

~

Never put a period where God has put a comma. —Gracie Allen

~

God seems to have left the receiver off the hook and time is running out.
-Arthur Koestler

~

On the wall of a rest stop on the Pennsylvania turnpike, someone scrawled the Scripture verse: "If God be for us who can be against us?" Someone else wrote, "The Cops."

~

One of the Waldensian Churches in Italy has a stained glass window which portrays several broken hammers scattered around an anvil. The inscription reads:

Hammer away ye hostile hands,
Your hammers break, God's anvil stands.

~

If your time ain't come, not even a doctor can kill you. –Proverb

~

It will all turn out in the end and if it doesn't, it isn't the end yet. -Brazilian proverb

~

Not for one single day
Can I discern my way,
But this I surely know-
Who gives the day,
Will show the way,
So I securely go.
-John Oxenham

~

In Enterprise, AL, there is a monument to the ever present pest which for decades ravaged Alabama's cotton fields. It reads, "In profound appreciation to the boll weevil and what it has done as the herald of prosperity." The success of the insect forced farmers to diversify their crops. Today peanuts are the leading agricultural crop in Enterprise.

~

Providence protects children and idiots. I know because I've tested it. —Mark Twain

~

I watched a foul ball at Memorial Stadium in Baltimore go high up in the second deck behind home plate. At that instant, a man was climbing the steps carrying a box of food with his back to the field of play. The ball hit in a seat just in front of him and gently popped up into the air. This lucky man simply reached out his hand, picked the soft bounce out of the air and went on to his seat. He never even broke stride and he never looked back. He was in the right place at the right time.

~

The Federal Register, October 25, 1979, page 61548 does some church and state work as it defines, *"An act of God." It's in regulation 50 CFR Part 258, Subpart C, Paragraph 285.21 (a). An act of God "means any act, event or circumstance ... whose effect could not reasonably have been prevented, avoided or ameliorated by human care, skill of foresight (either before or after the act, event, or circumstance) or a type, degree and timeliness which would normally be expected from an ordinarily prudent person in the same situation and under the prevailing circumstances."* Tell that to Moses, the Apostles, and the Lord.

~

A gentleman, reading the evening newspaper and the usual assortment of bad news, turns philosophical and says to his wife as she sets the table, "Isn't it amazing. The papers carry nothing but bad news. But, every day babies are born, the tides ebb and flow, and the sun will come up tomorrow morning at exactly 6:14 AM"

~

In the comic strip, "Miss Peach" by Mel Lazarus, Miss Peach turns to Arthur and asks, "Arthur, of all the eternal questions posed since time began, which has the most elusive answer of all?" Arthur responds, "Who's in charge here?"

~

Gerald Healy's play, "The Black Stranger", is set in Ireland in the awful days of the famine in the 19th Century. The government, in an effort to try and provide some work and income for the citizens, hired men to build roads, but the roads had no particular destination. One of the characters, Michael, came home from work one evening and sadly reported to his father, "They are making roads that lead nowhere."

~

A young soldier who returned from the war in Africa was asked by a woman to tell of his experiences. "Something must have happened," she declared. "Now tell me in all your experiences in Africa, what was it that struck you most?" "Well, ma'am," he began, "the thing that struck me the most was the amount of bullets that missed me." -"Sunday School Times"

~

One summer, Bishop Fiske wrote of spending a vacation with three of his friends and an old Maine fisherman guide. It was the summer when William Jennings Bryan was making his last attempt at the presidency and rock-ribbed Republican Maine was worried. One of the men in the party was a research physician; one was a geologist, and the other was an astronomer. They talked about the ages of the rocks and the evolution of life from the creatures of the sea and the immeasurable distance of the stars, and the old fisherman listened. At last he broke his silence and poured out a flood of questions. Were the rocks really so old? Did life evolve from the sea creatures? Were the stars so far away? Was everything so inconceivably vast and ancient? And when at last he got it in his mind, he heaved a sigh of relief. "I guess," he said, "it won't make a powerful lot of difference even if William Jennings Bryan is elected President."

-Harry Emerson Fosdick

~

The longer I live the more convincing proofs I see that God governs in the affairs of man; and if a sparrow cannot fall to the ground without his notice, is it probable that an empire can rise without his aid? -Ben Franklin

~

Prior to serving the Chinese community in Osaka, Japan, Kenneth Wilson was a missionary in Yinsien, China. At the beginning of the Second World War, a Japanese soldier by the name of Mizukami showed up at his house and asked if he could see the Mission Hospital, the Church, and the school. He had never seen a Christian institution before. Mr. Wilson showed him around and invited him into his home for tea. Then he gave him a Bible and prayed for him. He never expected to see Mizukami-san again. In 1966, 27 years later, he received a post card from a minister in northern Japan asking if he were the Kenneth Wilson who used to live in Yinsien, China. He said that Mizukami-san was in his inquirers' class and would soon be professing his faith in Jesus Christ. Mizukami-san told him about a very kind Mr. Kenneth Wilson who gave him a Bible and prayed for him back in 1939.

~

PURPOSE

A father and his little girl were on a long bus tour of the city. She asked, "Daddy, where will we be when we get where we want to go?"

~

A toast to the broker: He keeps us poor all our lives so we can die rich.

~

Some spend their health to gain wealth. Then they spend their wealth to regain their health.
                                                                      – Unknown

~

I blunder, I bluster, I blow, and I blother.
I make on the one day
and I mar on the other.
–John Skelton 1460-1529

~

With a good conscience our only sure reward, with history the final judge of our deeds; Let us go forth to lead the land we love, asking God's blessing and His help, but knowing that here on earth, God's work must truly be our own.
                                      --President John F. Kennedy, Inaugural Address

~

An old church in Belgium hired an artist to spruce up some artwork that had faded through the years. He sent back a bill for $22.50. The church officers thought that was too costly and requested an itemized statement. Back it came:
    Correcting the Ten Commandments, $5.13
    Renewing heaven and adjusting the stars, $7.14
    Touching up purgatory and restoring souls, $3.06
    Brightening up the flames of hell and doing odd jobs for the damned, $7.17.
I've had members who believed the world was in such a mess that about all we can hope to do is some odd jobs for the damned.

~

Not all roads lead to the peak of the same mountain; some lead over the precipice.
                                                              -William Sloane Coffin

~

Poor Richard's Almanac includes this thought: The noblest question in the world is, "What good can I do in it?"

~

A little bird built a comfortable nest low in the fork of a tree. She worked hard building a nice nest and in a few weeks she hatched her young. When they were only a few days old, a tomcat came along and easily climbed up to the nest and ate the little birds. The mother bird flew frantically about scolding the cat, but there was nothing she could do. Another bird came by and said, "I'm sorry, little bird, I'm sorry, but you built your nest too close to the ground." (I forgot whether it was the mother bird or the tom cat who told me this story.)

~

Unhappiness is not knowing what you want and killing yourself to get it.

~

There are two beginnings to every person's life. The first is the day one is born. The second is the moment when one discovers why one was born.

~

"Our statistics tell us our children are not being baptized, our people are not being nurtured, our members are not attending worship and communion regularly. Many of us wouldn't go around the corner to win a convert, but our leaders will encompass land and sea to attend a meeting and our members will assemble from British Columbia to Newfoundland to organize another committee." -   -A.C. Forrest, "United Church of Christ Observer"

~

When Henry Aaron first stepped up to bat as a little known rookie for the Milwaukee Braves, the catcher razzed him. "Hey, kid, you're holding your bat wrong. You're supposed to hold it so you can read the label." Henry Aaron replied, "I didn't come up here to read."

~

THE PURPOSE OF A LIFE IS A LIFE OF PURPOSE. -Robert Byrne

~

The good Lord didn't create anything without a purpose, but the fly comes close.
-Mark Twain

~

Here lived decent,
godless people.
Their only monument,
The asphalt road
and a million lost
golf balls."
-T.S. Eliot

~

I LIKE LIFE. IT'S SOMETHING TO DO. --Ronnie Shakes

~

You have to decide whether you want to make money or make sense, because the two are mutually exclusive.   -R. Buckminster Fuller

~

He who has a why to live for can bear with any how. -Frederick Nietzsche

~

Isn't love grand! You can see that spark in their eyes as they "discover" one another. They've both recently graduated with honors in their MBA program. Today, they are hand in hand on the beach. She looks deep into his eyes and says, "Oh, John, this is so wonderful. I love you so much and we have so much in common. I also want a million dollars before I'm thirty and a dream house on the beach."

~

Great minds have purposes, others have wishes. –Washington Irving

~

The husband was down in the dumps. "I have nothing to live for," he says. His wife replies, "That's the stupidest thing I've ever heard. Look at this place. The house, the car, the boat--none of them paid for. What more could you want to live for?"

~

Someone asked Hillary as he prepared to climb Mt. Everest, if he really wanted to go through with it. Hillary replied, "If you have to ask the question, you will never understand the answer."

~

In one "Peanuts" cartoon, Lucy says to Charlie Brown, "Charlie Brown, I think I am going to try and begin some new hobbies." Charlie Brown, in his usual way replies, "That's wonderful Lucy, that's a great idea. The people that get the most out of life are those who accomplish something." Lucy seems shocked. She says, "Accomplish something? Why, I thought we were just supposed to be busy."

-Charles M. Shulz

~

Two old fellows were asked, "What would you do differently if you had your lives to live over?" They thought for several minutes before answering. One took a deep breath, frowned, and said, "I'd grow a mustache." The next guy replied, "I'd part my hair on the left."

~

All things have their uses and their part and proper place in nature's economy: the ducks eat the flies; the flies eat the worms; the Indians eat all three. The wildcats eat the Indians; the white folks eat the wildcats; and thus all things are lovely."

-Mark Twain, "Roughing It"

~

Poet, novelist, and former President of Czechoslovakia, Vaclav Havel, said, "The tragedy of modern humanity is not that we know less and less about the meaning of life, but that it bothers us less and less."

~

When I moved to the Washington, DC, area in 1974, it was necessary for me to attain a higher level of sophistication. Prior to that time, I called a street which had no exit, a "dead-end street." I quickly learned from persons who lived in such places that the proper name for the street was a "cul-de-sac." If I lived on one, I'd probably call it a cul-de-sac too, but, in all honesty, "a dead-end street" is much more descriptive. But you don't have to live on a cul-de-sac to be on a dead-end street. I know lots of people who live on one.

~

REIGN OF GOD (Society)*

Tolstoy once told an eager young reformer, "Young man, you sweat too much blood for the world; sweat some for yourself first. . .If you want to make the world better you have to be the best you can be. .You cannot bring the Kingdom of God into the world until you bring it into your own heart.

~

A prayer that makes no mention of the kingdom is no prayer at all.   -The Talmud

~

If one really believes in God, not a theoretical analysis of deity but in a basic Fact which makes the universe moral through and through—then he may be sure that ought and can are twins. To say that what ought to be done cannot be done is a brief but complete confession of atheism; one who says that does not believe in God.
                                                            -Harry Emerson Fosdick

~

Do you or your church really mean it when you declare, "Jesus is Lord"? It is an easy affirmation to make; the words just roll off the tongue so smoothly and sound so pious. There are those who mouth these wonderful sounding words, but immediately start making caveats and qualifying this basic affirmation of Christian faith. The Presbyterian Church, USA, in its "Confession of 1967" declares that "the redeeming work of Jesus Christ embraces the whole of human life; social and cultural, economic and political, scientific and technological, individual and corporate; and environmental." If one really believes that, is there any area of human experience which is off limits for Jesus, the Lord of all?

~

"Twenty years ago in my most extravagant mood, I could not have dared to say to Christ, 'Let me live to see slavery destroyed'; and yet I have lived to see it destroyed. One such coronation lived through, I should indeed be most unreasonable to ask to live through any more such victories. . I shall die before I see commerce and industry fairly regenerated. Some of you will live to see the beginnings of it. But I foresee it. I preach it. My word will not die when I am dead. The seed has sprouted and you cannot unsprout it."   -Henry Ward Beecher

~

A fascinating character in our nation's early literature is Rip Van Winkle who lay down in the Catskill mountains for a nap and slept for twenty years. What would it be like to be middle aged and wake up an old man with your wife dead and buried and your little girl married with children of her own? Yet, the most amazing thing about Rip Van Winkle is that he slept right through a revolution.

~

* See also PROVIDENCE

The minister asked the junior high Sunday school class, "What is the Kingdom of God?" One young man volunteered, "I think it's God's tomorrow, which is kind of here today already."

-Leonard T. Wolcot, "Alive Now"

~

Leonard Bernstein says in one of his songs in "West Side Story"--"the air is humming for something great is coming".

~

During the depression, New York's famous Mayor Fiorello LaGuardia was presiding in night court when a man was found guilty of stealing a loaf of bread. The man said he needed the bread to feed his family. "The law is the law," said LaGuardia, "I must fine you ten dollars." But the accused said, "I don't have any money." LaGuardia took ten dollars out of his wallet and tossed it into the famous big hat he used to wear. "Mr. Bailiff, here's the fine. Now I am fining every person in this courtroom fifty cents for living in a city where a poor man must steal a loaf of bread in order to feed his family. Collect the fines and give them to this man." The man left the courtroom that night with more than $40.00 in his pocket, walking as if in a trance.

~

Victor Hugo, struggling with demons within, wrote: "Will the future ever arrive? Shall we continue to look upwards? Is the light we can see in the sky one of those which will presently be extinguished? The ideal is terrifying to behold, lost as it is in the depths, small, isolated, a pin point, brilliant, but threatened on all sides by the dark forces that surround it; and then he adds, "Nevertheless, no more in danger than a star in the jaws of the clouds."

~

While we deliberate, He reigns; when we decide wisely, He reigns; when we decide foolishly, He reigns; when we serve Him in humble loyalty, He reigns; when we serve Him self-assertedly, He reigns; when we rebel and seek to withhold our services, He reigns, the Alpha and Omega, which is and which was and which is to come, the Almighty.

–William Temple

~

One evening Benjamin Franklin's mother called him for supper. But he didn't come. His mother went to his room to find him with his face pressed against the window pane. He was watching the lamplighter go from post to post lighting the lamps on the city square. "Benjamin, what are you doing?" she asked. He replied, "Momma, it's so much fun to sit here and watch the lamplighter punch holes in the darkness."

~

Once a student of Tolstoy was hauled into court for refusing military service. When he defended himself by quoting from the Gospels, the judge said impatiently, "But, son, you are talking about the Kingdom of Heaven, and that hasn't come yet." The young man replied, "Sir, it may not have come for you, but it has come for me"

-Charles Wallis, *A Treasure of Sermon Illustrations*

~

Prophet: A person who gets to know what God is thinking.   –A child's definition

~

One gets no music from a violin when its strings are not tight. When the athlete is not tense for the contest he is not ready. The horse that is not nervous in the gate will never win a race. When the cables on a bridge are not tight enough to sing, it is condemned. Good friend, if you have tension between what is and what ought to be, consider yourself blessed and happy! It is a sure sign of God's presence and God's confidence in you. It is proof positive that God is working on you and through you; it is God's nudge for you to put muscle and brain behind your prayer that God's Kingdom would come on earth as it is in heaven.

~

Richard Hudnut in his book, *The Sleeping Giant,* said of suburbanites: "They are people who want to live in a microcosm of the Kingdom of God where the major enemy is crabgrass."

~

Society is made up of two great classes; those who have more dinners than appetite, and those who have more appetite than dinners.
                                            –Sabastian Rock Nicolas Chamfort, 1741-1794

~

I'll never forget going to the 1964 World's Fair in New York City where the US built a beautiful pavilion to showcase the plans for what was then our vision of "The Great Society." My wife and I had walked a considerable distance to see it; but when we rounded the corner, we were met with a huge sign which read, "Closed."

~

To get into the best society nowadays, one has either to feed people, amuse people, or shock people.
                                            –Oscar Wilde

~

There are three classes of citizens. The first are the rich, who are indolent and yet always crave more. The second are the poor, who have nothing, are full of envy, hate the rich, and are easily led by demagogues. Between the two extremes lie those who make the state secure and uphold the laws.   –Euripides 420 BCE

~

As a crowd of well-dressed theater-goers approached The Kennedy Center they passed two homeless persons sitting on a bench. They all gave one another the once over. And these words were overheard: "Get a good look at them and you find out what's wrong with this country!" But, who said it? It's a mystery.

~

After being bounced out of the side exit of the Willard Hotel, the man said indignantly, "Look here, mister, I belong to one of the most important families in this city." The doorman was shocked. He apologized profusely and invited him back inside. Then he threw him out the front door.

~

Cockroaches and socialites are the only things that can stay up all night and eat anything.
                                            -Herb Caen

~

SALVATION

A man announced that he was saved. A friend asked him how long he had been in that blessed state. His reply: "About twenty years, off and on."

~

A woman was overheard at Disneyland telling her small son, "Now, I'm warning you, if you get lost, don't come crying to me." Maybe she said that right after her ride on Space Mountain. But, just suppose her son was lost. She'd give everything she owned to have her boy come crying back to her.

~

Moses and the Israelites are crossing over the Red Sea. Before their eyes a wall of water is held back. Moses says to a chronic complainer, "Yes, thanks for your help. It is damp."

~

"We Christians talk about saving the world. That is not disturbing. That even sounds beautiful. We can put that into poetry and sing it. I can preach about it so you can go out and say how pleasing it is to think about the world being saved. My friends, alter the phrase. We cannot save this world without changing it. And when we speak of changing it, that has another sound. (It is almost foreboding.) We cannot save our international relationships without changing them. We cannot save our economic system without changing it. We cannot save ourselves without being changed, radically changed. Sometimes I think we would do well to declare a moratorium on the world "save."

-Harry Emerson Fosdick, from a sermon entitled, "Hope and Change"

~

Now, therefore, we declare, say, determine and pronounce that for every human creature it is necessary for salvation to be subject to the authority of the Roman pontiff.

-Pope Boniface VIII, 1235-1303

~

In high school some of my friends wanted to know if I were "saved." The adult leader of a Bible Study Group asked me, "Do you know Jesus and do you know that if you died tonight you would go to heaven? Are you totally and completely sure about that?" I replied, "No, I'm not completely sure". He responded, "Would you like to know without a shadow of a doubt that you would go to heaven if you died?" My answer was, "Well, of course I would." We went into another room where the lights were turned down low. All of us in the class joined hands and everyone in the circle prayed that Jimmy would know without a shadow of a doubt that he was saved and that he would go to heaven when he died. After the last Amen, everyone opened their eyes and looked at me. "Well, do you know now?" They asked. . . I lied. "Yeah, I really know now." It was the only way I could get home.

~

O Lord—if there is a Lord; save my soul—if I have a soul. Amen.
-Joseph Renan, Prayer of a Skeptic 1823-1890

"Customized Salvation." -Sign at nondenominational church in Miami Beach

~

God's arithmetic: sin subtracted; grace added; gifts divided; and peace multiplied.

~

Somewhere I read about an Eskimo hunter who asked the local missionary priest, if he did not know about God and sin, would he go to hell? The priest told him "No, not if you didn't know." "Then why," inquired the Eskimo, "did you tell me?"

~

In the southwest a great flood threatened the whole region and heroic people were going from house to house rescuing folks from the impending disaster. When a truck arrived at the house of a devout Texan, he refused to leave, saying, "The Lord is my refuge. God will deliver me." The next day a big strong fellow came in a boat. "Hurry, sir, the water is rising, and it's too dangerous for you to remain here." The Texan said, "I'm a believer and the Lord has promised to deliver me." The next day the water was almost up to the roof. The man was clinging to the chimney. A helicopter hovered overhead and lowered a rope ladder to the Texan. But he refused to take the rope. "The Lord will deliver me," he said. In heaven he had several complaints for the Almighty. "Lord, you promised to deliver all those who trust in You. I trusted in you and you let me die in a flood. Why didn't you deliver me?" The Lord replied, "What more can you ask of me? I sent you a truck, a boat, and a helicopter and you wouldn't ride in any of them."

~

In the comic strip, "Peanuts", Rerun is in agony and Lucy tries to comfort him. "Stop crying, Rerun, have a cookie!" In the next frame Rerun is clutching the cookie and looking longingly at it as Lucy lectures, "Just remember this, Rerun, the day is coming when a cookie will not solve all your problems." The last frame shows Rerun taking a bite out of the cookie and with a big smile, he says, "Until then."

~

Martin Marty told of a soul winner who felt it his responsibility to inquire about everyone's salvation. He'd ask, "Are you born again?" Sometimes he'd shorten it to, "Are you B.A.?" One individual responded, "No I'm not B.A., I'm B.S. in engineering."

-"Context"

~

Remember that great cowboy, Roy Rogers, who rode Trigger and crooned cowboy songs? He used to sing, "O give me land, lots of land under starry skies above, don't fence me in." I doubt if Roy was aware he was crooning "good theology". Hear the Psalmist: "I cried to the Lord in my distress and the Lord answered me and set me in a large place. (KJV)" In that large place there are no fences and one is free to move about and be constantly surprised by new experiences of grace, new thoughts, new dreams.

~

SECOND COMING

"Jesus is coming soon, perhaps tomorrow. Send $20.00 for these tapes that explain the second coming of Christ. Please allow six weeks for delivery." — TV commercial

~

From the Did You Notice Dept: Most of the signs along the roadside which remind us Jesus is coming soon are made of reinforced concrete blocks?

~

Bill Jarrett, in his ordination exam in Orange Presbytery, NC, was asked if he were a post-millenialist or a pre-millenialist. Bill astounded the Presbytery by announcing he was a "*pan-millenialist*." The Reverend in charge of Theology was stunned. Expecting a long theological discussion, he asked, "What do you **mean** 'pan-millenialist'? Bill replied, "I believe it's all going to pan out in the end." Examination sustained!

~

An agnostic announced, "Due to a lack of trained trumpeters, the end of the world has been postponed indefinitely."

~

When Cardinal Basil Hume of London was asked how he would celebrate the millennium replied, "I'll be splashing around in the fountains of Trafalgar Square with everyone else."

~

In Parker's, "The Wizard of Id", Lester is carrying a doom's day sign, "The world will end one of these days. . .perhaps." One observer comments, "I'm afraid Lester's conversion has been something less than total."

~

Returning from a long revival meeting, the son asked his father, "Daddy, what is a millennium?" The father replied, "Son, it's the same as a centennial except it has more legs."

~

JESUS IS COMING. LOOK BUSY. –Bumper Sticker

~

I have no idea when Jesus is coming back. I'm on the Welcoming Committee, not the Planning Committee. -Tony Campolo

~

If some of these folks would spend their time following Jesus example instead of trying to figure out His mode of arrival and departure, they would come nearer getting confidence in their church. -Will Rogers

~

When the trumpet of the Lord shall sound…I'm outta here. –Bumper Sticker

~

When the rapture comes I want to be in Cincinnati. They are always 50 years behind.
                                    -Mark Twain
When the rapture comes this car will be unmanned. –Bumper Sticker

~

When the rapture comes, can I have your car? -Bumper Sticker

~

The son asked, "How did the preacher know Jesus was ruptured?" Mother said, "Honey, it's raptured."

~

If it is the end of all time, the last moment, and you have a seedling—go ahead and plant it.
                                    –Arab saying

~

A faith healer went to a town in southwest Texas and preached a week of rousing sermons on Jesus' Second Coming. On the last night he preached convincingly that the Lord would return that very week. Then he asked for a show of hands of those who believed that Jesus would return this very week. Almost every hand went up. "You're right," he said. "And if Jesus comes this very week you're not going to need the money you have in the bank. Remember that as the ushers pass the offering plates."

~

One afternoon when I was in the fifth grade in Detroit, MI, I sat nervously with my classmates waiting for the end of the world. The papers carried news articles of a religious group which claimed special revelation that the world would end at 2:00 PM that afternoon. We were scared and watched the clock until 2:05 until we were sure the prediction was wrong and we could all breathe a collective sign of relief.

~

When Jesus spoke about his coming again, He said He would be "coming on the clouds of heaven" (Matthew 26:64). We have only to ask the question which naturally follows to see how absurd it would be to take such a statement literally: *Where* will he appear on the clouds? Palestine? New York? Alabama? South Africa? The point is obviously not *how* and *where* he will come, but *that* God in Christ will be the Judge and Saviour of all people at the end of history.
Paul pictures Christ coming "with the sound of the trumpet of God" (1Thessalonians 4:16). His point is surely not that God will blow a trumpet, but that a great victory is coming.
                                    –Shirley Guthrie, Christian Doctrine

~

SEEKING*

Einstein was once asked how he worked. He replied, "I grope."

~

Keep on going and the chances are you will stumble on something. Perhaps when you are least expecting it. I have never heard of anyone's stumbling on something sitting down.
                                                                      -Charles F. Kettering

~

Thomas Edison worked tirelessly to develop the electric light. After an exhausting day, his assistant was discouraged and said, "This day has been a waste. "Edison responded, "Not at all. We now know 70 things that won't work."

~

The voice over the telephone was obviously that of a child.

Man: Is your Daddy home?
Child: Yes.
Man: Can I talk to him?
Child: No, He's busy.
Man: Well, is your Mommy there?
Child: Yes.
Man: Can I talk to **her**?
Child: No, whispered the child, She's busy.
Man: Is there any other adult there?
Child: Yes. There's a policeman and a firemen here too.
Man: Well, would you let me talk to **them?**
Child: No, they're busy.
Man: Well, what is everybody doing?
Child: They're looking for me.

~

A man yearned to see Mohammed in his dreams but was never successful. He sought the advice of a devout friend who said, "My son, on Friday evening eat a lot of salt fish, then say your prayers and go to bed. But don't drink any water. Then you will see Mohammed in your dreams.

He followed his friend's instructions and dreamed all night long about drinking from streams and fountains. In the morning he rushed to his friend and said, "I didn't see Mohammed. I was so thirsty all I dreamed about was drinking water." I'm still thirsty."

Said the devout friend, "So eating salt fish gave you such a great thirst that you dreamed only of water? Now go and feel such a great thirst for Mohammed and you will see him in your dreams."
                                                                      -Ancient Sufi story

~

* See also PREPARATION

Watching the coast as it slips by the ship is like thinking about an enigma. There it is before you -- smiling, frowning, inviting, grand, mean, insipid or savage, and always a mute air of whispering, "Come and find out."   –Joseph Conrad, *Heart of Darkness*

~

Stanley Bing, writing on his spiritual quest, says, "I tried to catch the Buddhism wave for a couple of days. It didn't really work. You have to sit for hours and hours and think about nothing. I normally get paid for that. And there are no guarantees such contemplation will pay off in anything more than a certain quiet satisfaction. Me, I'm looking for ecstasy. So I moved on."   –Fortune Magazine, 11/10/97

~

Parents in every culture play hide and seek with their children. "You can come look for me now, I'm hiding." And mommy or daddy starts searching. "Hmmm, I wonder where my little girl is? Where can she be?" As if you didn't know. You can always find those kids, can't you mom and dad? Because you **are** the mom and dad and it is your job to find them, no matter where they are. When you find them they are joyously happy. They love it. It's so good to be found by mom and dad.

~

Rebbe Barukh's grandson, Yehiel, came running into his study in tears. Yehiel, why are you crying?" "My friend cheats! It's unfair; he left me all by myself. That's why I am crying." Would you like to tell me about it?" asked the Rebbe.

"We played hide and seek and it was my turn to hide and his turn to look for me. So he gave up; he stopped looking. And that's unfair." Rebbe began to caress Yehiel's face, and tears welled up in his eyes. "God too," Yehiel," he whispered softly. "God too is unhappy; he is hiding and people are not looking for him. Do you understand, Yehiel? God is hiding and man is not even searching for him."

--Hasidic tale

~

One of the most dramatic acts of the famous German clown, Karl Vallentin, was to enter the stage as all the lights went off. Amidst that darkness one solitary street light came on. Valletin would desperately look for something under the light. A policeman enters and asks what he is looking for? The clown answers, "The key to my house." The two of them then search in earnest for the key. The policeman asks, "Are you sure this is where you lost it?" Vallentin replies, "Oh, no, I lost it over there," pointing to a dark corner of the stage. The policeman asks, "Then why are you looking for it over here?" Vallentin replies, "Because there is no light over there."

~

You are mistaken if you think I do not believe in God. . . I seek God in man, in human freedom, and now I seek God in revolution.

–Mikhail A. Bakunin, Russian writer, 1814-1876

STRESS*

"EVEN IF YOU WIN THIS RAT RACE, YOU'RE STILL A RAT!"

Psychiatrists tell us the people who are able to endure stress are those who know their own limitations and know when to say, "To hell with it."

~

Said the Red Queen in Lewis Carroll's *Through the Looking Glass*, "It takes all the running you can do to keep in the same place. If you want to get somewhere else, you must run at least twice as fast as that!"

~

America has been so tense and nervous it's been years since I've seen someone asleep in church--and that's a bad situation.　　　　　-Norman Vincent Peale

~

A woman's psychiatrist advised her to stay away from those things that give her stress. So she doesn't open the psychiatrist's bills anymore.　　　–Unknown

~

In his later years, the composer, Brahms, was greatly stressed. He confided to a friend that the music just wouldn't come. Then he thought: I'm an old man, why should I write any more at all. I'll just enjoy life. That spirit relaxed him so much the music just flowed.　　　　　　–Unknown

~

You have to fight fleas even when fighting elephants.　　-African proverb

~

Reality is the leading cause of stress. I can take it in small doses, but as a life style I find it too confusing.　　　　–Jane Wagner, *The Search for Intelligent Life in the Universe*

~

* See also *ANXIETY (TENSION)*

In Joseph Heller's novel, *Something Happened*, the boss, Jack Green, makes it clear what he expects from his subordinates. He doesn't want "good work" but "spastic colitis and nervous exhaustion." Says he, *"Damn it, I want the people working for me to be worse off than I am, not better. That's the reason I pay you so well. I want to see you right on the verge. I want it right out in the open. I want to be able to hear it in a stuttering, flustered, tongue-tied voice ... Don't trust me. I don't want trust, flattery, loyalty and sociability. I don't trust deference, respect and cooperation. I trust fear."* If you work for anyone resembling, Mr. Jack Green, I guarantee you will be stressed out!

-Christopher Lasch. *The Culture of Narcissism*

~

You don't get ulcers from what you eat. You get them from what's eating you.

-Vicki Baum

~

STRESSED SPELLED BACKWARDS = DESSERTS.

~

God never built a Christian strong enough to carry today's duties and tomorrow's anxieties piled on the top of them. 　　　　　　　　　-Theodore Ledyard Cuyler

~

No one ever became a saint in ones sleep.

~

Litter bugs me. -Bumper Sticker

~

When my grandson, Woody, was four years old he was working on loving his little sister and it didn't come easily. He had his four-year-old moments and his four-year-old problems. When the family was decorating the Christmas tree, he remarked she should be put in the closet. Shortly thereafter, and holding the TV remote control, he pointed it at his one-year-old rival who was crawling toward him, and said, "Roxana, I'm going to turn you off." Come to think of it, wouldn't that be a great invention?

~

FOR FAST ACTING RELIEF TRY SLOWING DOWN. -Lily Tomlin

~

A diamond is a chunk of coal that made good under pressure. -Unknown

~

We all choke and the man who says he doesn't choke is lying like hell. We all leak oil.

-Lee Trevino, golf professional

~

I try to take one day at a time, but sometimes several days attack me at once.

-Ashleign Brilliant

~

TIME*

The first one to see the traffic light turn green is the second car back. -MacGregor's Law

~

Arthur Arch, an Englishman, had just turned 95 years old. But the important thing about Arthur Arch was that for 42 years he had been precisely 20 minutes late for any meeting or appointment he had. It was not about being prompt. He was precisely prompt. However, he was always 20 minutes late. He reported that as a result, he had been fired a half dozen times and missed a great many trains, which, in England, usually run on time. When asked why he was always 20 minutes late, he said, "It's very simple, really. In 1922, the clocks were adjusted and changed 20 minutes. I never accepted this. Nobody was going to take 20 minutes off of my life. I have just always kept my watch at the old time -- 20 minutes late." Arthur Arch vowed that he was never going to change his clocks to be in step with the world. Said he, "I'm going to die 20 minutes late to show them that I was right."
-Hoover Rupert, "Presbyterian Outlook" 1/21/80

~

How many people want to live forever but don't know what to do with themselves on a rainy day.

~

Among those things which are not what they used to be are us. -Howard Kirksey

~

After hearing his coach speak on the importance of graduating from college, a new freshman vowed to graduate on time no matter how long it takes.

~

In reality, killing time is only the name for another of the multifarious ways by which time kills us.   -Sir Osbert Sitwell, 1892-1969

~

The plumber was late getting to the house to fix the leak. "I hope you've managed OK." he said. The man of the house responded, "It hasn't been all that bad. We just taught the kids how to swim."   -Unknown

~

We spend our time ignoring the years and focusing on particular moments.

~

The trouble with being punctual is there is no one there to appreciate it.
-"Journal of Religious Speaking"

~

The waiter took his order for some clam chowder. After considerable time he returned with the soup. The customer inquired, "Are you the same waiter that took my order?" "Yes, why?" asked the waiter. The man replied, "That's funny, you looked much younger then."

~

* See also HISTORY

Time is the wisest of all counselors.   —Plutarch

~

A father and his five year old son were watching a TV Western. As the story reached its climax, with the cowboy hero facing the fastest gun in the West, the youngster got up and turned off the TV and went out of the room. "Hey, why did you turn that off?" his father demanded. The boy replied, "I have to go to the bathroom and I don't want to miss anything."

~

After the waiter looked right through him for the third time, he wrote, An Ode To the Waiter: "Bye and bye, God caught his eye!"   -Unknown

~

No man is rich enough to buy back his past.   -Oscar Wilde

~

While a student at Union Theological Seminary, I worked at the Virginia State Penitentiary. Along with another student, we were responsible for leading worship. One Sunday morning, because the chaplain was late in arriving, we led a hymn sing. We were anxious that the men might be restless and not want to sing any longer, so my colleague rather apologetically suggested, "The chaplain isn't here yet. Why don't we sing another hymn or two? Have you got a minute?" A burly fellow on the front row replied, "Have I got a **minute**? I got twenty years."

~

We really need a new name for "rush hour". That's the only time of day when you can't rush.

~

Igor Stravinsky, the composer, was a hard worker and strict disciplinarian when it came to his work schedule. When his publisher once told him to hurry and finish his composition, Stravinsky was furious. "Hurry, did you say? I never hurry! I don't have time to hurry!"   -Unknown

~

Time is a great teacher. Unfortunately it kills all its pupils. -Hector Berlioz

~

When Noah sailed the waters blue,
He had his troubles same as you;
For forty days he drove the ark
Before he found a place to park.
-Author unknown

~

With God time is eternity in disguise. -Abraham Heschel

~

When Larry Rasmussen served as a missionary in Africa, he received a cable informing him to go to another city as soon as possible. He checked the train schedule, got into his car and bounced to the station at N'Garoundere. He jumped out and pursued the train which was just pulling away from the station. The conductor yelled to him as he ran toward the train, "Take your time, take your time. There's lots of time. This is yesterday's train."

Time: that which is simultaneously marching on and running out.

~

Dr. Christy Wilson, former Presbyterian Missionary to Afghanistan, was seated in an old DC-3 on the runway in Kabul when the stewardess locked the door. Then they sat for a long time until there was a knock at the door. "Let me in. Let me in," cried an anxious voice. The stewardess said, "I can't. We are forbidden to open the door. We are getting ready to take off." Again the voice: "You will not take off. I'm the pilot."

~

There's really not a whole lot of time between a green banana and a mushy one.

~

When one of the engines on the 737 conked out on a flight from Kansas City to Washington, the pilot said over the loudspeaker, "We will be 40 minutes late, but don't worry, this plane is built to fly on only one engine." A passenger turned to his seat mate and said, "I hope the other one doesn't go out. No telling how late we'd be."

~

Time is nature's way of keeping everything from happening all at once. –Unknown

~

Kiki Cuyler of the Chicago Cubs had a powerful throwing arm when he played right field. In one game against the New York Giants, he cut down Travis Jackson trying to score from second base on a single to right. As Pancho Snyder, the Giant's third base coach, passed the Cub's bench they gave him the business. "How'd you like that throw, Pancho?" "He couldn't do it again in a hundred years," he growled back. A few innings later Cuyler again cut down Jackson at the plate. The Cub's hollered from the dugout, "Hey, Pancho, time sure flies, eh?"

-Herman Masin, Curve Ball Laughs

~

Time flies, you say? No, not really. We fly, time stays. –Unknown

~

When the speedster took a long lead off first base, the pitcher turned and threw. Desperately, the runner dove back head first and shouted, "I made it, I made it." The umpire replied philosophically, "Yes, you did, son. You made it, but you were late."

~

There can't be a crisis next week. My schedule is already full. -Henry Kissinger

~

The wife programmed her answer machine which played just as her husband climbed in bed. "I'm sorry I cannot answer you personally right now, but after the beep, if you'll leave your name and number and a brief message, I'll get back with you as soon as I can. Now here's the beep."

~

There's never time to do it right, but always time to do it over. –Proverb

~

You can get anywhere in ten minutes if you go fast enough. –Unknown

~

TRUST

When I was young, service station attendants *always* cleaned your windshield, checked your oil and water, and, if requested, the air pressure in your tires. Nowadays, if you *ask* them to check under the hood, I guarantee that they will find something that needs to be fixed immediately.

~

In God we trust. All others pay cash. -Sign in gas station

~

Two guys in prison were explaining why they were doing time. One said, "I'm here because I trusted everybody." The other said, "I'm here because I didn't trust anybody."

~

Would a sheep notice a shepherd who wears a sheepskin vest?"

~

It is painfully obvious that the person who closes on the bank loan is not the same person who wrote the TV ad.

~

Who mistrusts most should be trusted least.   --Greek proverb

~

It is equally an error to trust all men or no man.   --Latin proverb

~

Don't trust anyone over thirty. -60's Slogan

~

TRUST EVERYONE BUT CUT THE CARDS.

~

I told you I was sick. -epitaph Lee Trevino wants on his tombstone

~

Depend on the rabbit's foot if you will, but remember it didn't work for the rabbit.
-R. E. Shay

~

There is a legend about some imps who met together to devise a plan to hide from humankind the thought that people could trust God. Their ingenious plan was to hide it where people would be least likely to look for it. They hid it deep in the human heart.

~

He who believes in nobody knows that he himself is not to be trusted. —Auerbach

~

The human heart, at whatever age, opens only to the heart that opens in return.
-Marie Edgeworth

~

You may be deceived if you trust too much, but you will live in torment if you don't trust enough.   —Frank Crane

~

In the book *Everybody Wins: Transactional Analysis Applied to Organizations*, there is the following free verse by Lyman K. Randall.

"Of Course I Believe"

Trust you?
Sure I trust you!
(I wonder what he's after now?)
Be open with you?
Of course, I'm open with you!
(As open as I can be with a guy like you.)
Level with you?
You know I level with you!
(I'd like to more, but you can't take it.)
Accept you?
Naturally I accept you -- just like you accept me.
(And when you learn to accept me, I might accept you more.)
Self direction?
I've always believed in self-direction!
(And some day this company may let us use some.)
What's the hang up?
Not a damn thing!
What could ever hang up
Two self-directing,
Open, trusting,
Leveling and accepting
Guys like us?

~

Coming into Harrisonburg, VA, is a huge sign that reads: Welcome to Harrisonburg, VA. IN GOD WE TRUST.   —Hawks Security Systems, Inc.

~

Men say women can't be trusted too far; women say men can't be trusted too near.
                                        –J. M. Braude

~

Are you going to trust me or believe your own lying eyes?   – Groucho Marx

~

I think that we may safely trust a good deal more than we do. We may waive just so much care of ourselves as we honestly bestow elsewhere.   —Henry David Thoreau

VIRGIN BIRTH

Several years ago the fourth grade class of the Second Presbyterian Church in Charleston, SC, wrote, directed, and presented a Christmas Pageant. The problem was the actors didn't stick with the script. The pageant opened with the scene at the inn as Joseph and Mary asked for a room overlooking Bethlehem.

Innkeeper: "Can't you see the 'No Vacancy' sign?"
Joseph: "Yes, but can't you see my wife is expecting a baby any minute?"
Innkeeper: "Well, that's not my fault."
Joseph: "Well, It's not my fault either." -David MacLennan, *Church Chuckles*

~

In another Charleston, WV, a similar problem arose. The young fellow playing the inn keeper was so sympathetic with the Virgin Mary that he tried to be as accommodating as possible. When Joseph and Mary inquired if he had a room, the young fellow replied, "Wow, are you lucky. We just had a cancellation."

~

Two sisters were looking at the painting of the Virgin Mary and the Baby Jesus. "But where's the father?" the younger one asked. "Oh, he's taking the picture," said the older girl.
—Unknown

~

A second grade Sunday School Class was drawing pictures of the Nativity scene. One boy drew a beautiful picture with all the usual characters. He also added a fat boy beside the manger. The teacher asked for an explanation: "That's Round John Virgin." The pilot, Pontius, was ready for the flight to Egypt.

~

Isn't it a great name for a maternity hospital? *The Immaculate Conception Hospital, Manila?*

~

An Anglican Church installed the most recent software and typed in entire liturgies for regular worship, marriages, and funerals. A woman whose name was Mary died. The liturgy printed in the bulletin gave thanks for God's servant, Mary. In good order The Apostle's Creed was recited by the congregation. The next person to die was a woman named Edna. The Secretary entered a prayer of thanksgiving for God's servant, Edna. Everything went smoothly at the funeral until the congregation recited the Apostle's Creed and their belief in Jesus Christ, who was born of the Virgin Edna.
—Unknown

~

A little girl asked her grandmother, "Which Virgin was the mother of Jesus: the Virgin Mary or the King James Virgin?"

~

Today God made the glorious virgin laugh, because from her is born our laughter. Laughter is born, Christ is born! Therefore, let us laugh and rejoice with the blessed Virgin because God has given us, in her, a cause for laughing and rejoicing.
-Anthony of Padua 1195-1231

~

WAITING*

The early bird *may* get the worm; but the second mouse gets the cheese.

~

In spite of theological rhetoric to the contrary, the doctrine most practiced by Presbyterians is procrastination.

~

What a friend we have in time: gives us babies; makes us wine;
Tells us what to take and leave behind. -Unknown

~

His doctor said to General Ethan Allen of Revolutionary War fame, "General, I fear the angels are waiting for you." Allen replied, "Waiting, are they? Well, damn 'em, let 'em wait."

~

You've seen this ingenious sign when the store was closed in the middle of the day: "Back in 15 minutes. Already been gone 10."

~

Visitors to the White House were waiting in line to sign the registration book. Three nuns were in front of a Jewish family whose son, Shelly, was tired of waiting. He eased ahead of the nuns and was about to sign the book when his mother said, "Wait till the nun signs, Shelly."   -Unknown

~

The less your influence, the longer the wait.

~

God is willing to wait 14 billion years before humans appear on the earth. But we want our kids to mature in 18 years. We want our careers to improve tomorrow. We want social justice to appear today. When we go to a therapist, we expect our lives to change in a matter of months. We need to learn the art of waiting, the spiritual discipline of living in hope.   —John Wimberly, Jr. Sermon fragment

~

Ms. Manners hates "call waiting". She says it is proof positive of the maxim, "Last come, first served."

~

Hurry up and wait. -Military Saying

~

When the poet Kathleen Norris was asked, 'What is the main thing a poet does?' She replied, "We wait."

~

For years now I've heard the word "Wait!" It rings in the ear of every Negro with piercing familiarity. This "Wait" has almost always meant "Never."
-M. L. King, Jr. *Letters From A Birmingham Jail*

~

All things come to those who wait—- as long as they keep working. –Unknown

~

* See also *PATIENCE*

Things may come to those who wait, but only those things that are left by those who hustle.   -Unknown

~

A famous doctor died and went to heaven and found himself at the end of a long line. He made his way to the desk and said, "There must be some mistake. I'm Dr. Jones and I'm at the end of a long line." St. Peter said, "I'm sorry, Dr. Jones, but here in heaven, no one is more important than any one else; please take your turn; have patience; we'll be with you as soon as possible."

Dr. Jones went to the end of the line again, but then thought perhaps St. Peter didn't realize that he was an MD. Again, he went to St. Peter's desk and said, "St. Peter, do you know that I am a surgeon, a medical doctor?" St. Peter said, "Yes, we knew that, Dr. Jones. We'll be with you as soon as we can." He returned to his place. But, looking through the gates, he saw a woman with a stethoscope around her neck. He rushed to the gates and shouted, "Oh, Dr! Dr. Robert Jones, here, University of Chicago Medical Hospital." But there was no reply. He asked St. Peter, "Who is that doctor in the white coat?" St. Peter said, "Oh, that's God. She likes to play doctor every now and then."

~

Karl Walenda, the father of the famous high-wire aerialist family, said, "When I'm on the high wire I am fully alive. Everything else is waiting."

~

The older we get, the fewer things seem worth waiting in line for.   -Will Rogers

~

After her first week in school, a little girl told her mother "I'm wasting my time in school. I can't read. I can't write and they won't let me talk."

~

A refugee couple arrived in the United States several years ago with one dream—to become citizens. Through much red tape and years of study, they patiently waited and hoped. Then one day the husband rushed into the kitchen with the long-awaited good news. "Anna, Anna" he shouted. "At last we are Americans!" "That's fine," replied the wife, tying her apron around him. "Now you wash the dishes."   –J.M. Braude

~

There's an old folk tale about the two ways to climb an oak tree. One way is to wrap your arms and legs around the rough, scaly bark and work to climb up higher as you end up with several cuts and bruises. This way you will lose a portion of your hide but the view will be pretty when you get to the top. The other way is to plant an acorn and sit on it.

~

Don't wait for the last Judgment. It takes place every day.   –Albert Camus, *The Fall*

~

WISDOM *

In Johnny Hart's cartoon, "B.C." he portrays two characters sitting on a hill looking up at the moon. One asks, "I wonder if man will ever conquer the moon?" The other responds, "Why not? We've conquered everything else." But the other replies, "Not quite ... there's still stupidity."

~

Half this game is 90 percent mental.   -Philadelphia Phillies Manager, Danny Ozark

~

An Ivy League administrative office described their publication. "The Banner is published weekly by the Office of Public Information, except four times a month in September and March; three times a month in February and April, Twice monthly in November, December, and May; and once monthly in January and June. No issues in July and August." But in October, they are really pushed to the wall.

~

80 percent of kindergarten children got the answer to this riddle. Only 17 percent of Stanford University Seniors got the answer. What is greater than God, more evil than the devil, the poor have it, the rich need it, and if you eat it you will die? Answer: Nothing

~

In three words I can sum up all I've learned about life. It goes on. −Erich Fromm

~

The English Department was discussing the differences between Charles Dickens and Henry James. One said of Dickens, "He always bit off more than he could chew." Of James, he said, "He always chewed more than he'd bitten off."

~

In Cherokee, NC, the tourist industry focuses on its Indian heritage. Many Native Americans earn a living making crafts, serving as guides and performing Indian dances. A tourist approached a young mother who had her child strapped to her back in a papoose. She spoke in slow, elementary English in order to communicate. "Baby, cute. Baby cute!" The woman kept a straight face and nodded her head. When the tourist left she said to her friend, "You know, some people will never learn, will they?"   --Blake Brinkerhoff

~

Nobody in football should be called a genius. A genius is a guy like Norman Einstein.   -Joe Theismann, Football analyst

~

"The Nuclear News Magazine" contained this word of wisdom: "The development of hydro power in the desert of North Africa awaits only the introduction of water." I had a suspicion about that myself.

~

*See also KNOWLEDGE

I'd rather keep my mouth shut and be thought a fool, than to open my mouth and remove all doubt.   —Attributed to Abraham Lincoln

~

The first step of wisdom is to know what is false.   -Latin Proverb

~

In a cannibal meat market a customer asked, "What's the special today?" "Brains," said the man behind the counter. Pointing to the case he said, "These are lawyer's brains at $4.75 a pound. Here in the back are doctor's brains at $6.00 per pound. And here's a real buy! These are preacher's brains for $7.50 a pound."   The customer said, "That's an outrageous price. $7.50 a pound for preacher's brains, the very idea!" "Sir," said the attendant, "Do you have any idea how many preachers it takes to get a pound of brains?"

~

Senator Thomas Reed in 1890, said, "All the wisdom in the world consists in shouting with the majority."

~

In the film on the dangers of nuclear war, "The day after," one of the doctors says, "Stupidity has a habit of getting its way."

~

"The International Civil Defense Organization Manual" advises "injuries due to the cold include all those due to lack of warmth." *I knew it!*

~

Hire a college student while they still know it all.   -Bumper Sticker

~

The biggest problem of our time is that our knowledge is far ahead of our wisdom.

~

Everyone knows that trades like farming, building, engineering, carpentry all need apprenticeship. But when it comes to the task of interpreting the Word of God, well, any old talkative granny, any old fellow in his dotage, any frothy intellectual will blithely dissect and expound it without bothering to take any lessons in it. This is a childish way of going on, this is circus stuff, to set up as master in your own ignorance. Indeed to let my spleen speak, it means that you don't even know what you don't know.
                                                   -Letter from Jerome to Paulinus, 394 AD.

~

Every person is entitled to be a damn fool for at least five minutes a day. One is wise when she or he does not exceed the limit.   —Unknown

~

When the stomach speaks, wisdom is silent. -Arab Proverb

~

He's a little man, that's his trouble. Never trust a man with short legs--brains too near their bottoms.
                                                   -Neil Coward

~

The strongest human instinct is to impart information, the second strongest is to resist it.
                                                   --Kenneth Graham

~

When Bozo, the famous clown of Ringling Brothers Circus, retired, he worked for The American Cancer Society. He always closed his show, "Bye, bye now--and be sure your doctor checks you for cancer." But Bozo did not listen to his own counsel and waited too long to have his first check up. His doctors discovered an advanced malignancy.

~

WISDOM COMES BY DISILLUSIONMENT. —George Santayana

~

While looking at a house, a man asked the real estate agent which direction was north. He explained that he didn't want the sun waking him up every morning. When the agent said that the sun has risen in the East since creation, he shook his head and said, "Oh, I don't keep up with that stuff."

~

After paying hundreds of dollars for another year's coverage with the exterminating company to keep the bugs out of our house, my wife and I ate dinner on the patio.

~

In the spring of 1997, a seventeen year old high school senior in California made national news when she achieved a perfect score of 800 on both the math and the language sections of the SAT tests and a perfect 8000 on the tough University of California Acceptance Index. Never before had anyone achieved such a feat. At her high school she was known as "Wonder Woman." In an interview with a reporter she was asked, "What is the meaning of life?" She replied, "I have no idea." Smart? Yes, indeed! Wise? Not now. We should all pray that she might gain wisdom.

~

We've got so much intelligence today we can't afford education. -Bumper Sticker

~

How to Catch a Porcupine: Approach the porcupine with a large galvanized tub held in front of you. Avoid his slapping tail and quickly place tub over the porcupine. Immediately sit on top of the tub. Now, you have something to sit on while you think up your next move.   -Poster in a Wisconsin Tavern

~

THE ART OF WISDOM IS IN KNOWING WHAT TO OVERLOOK. —Unknown

~

It really doesn't help my wife to know intellectually that my soft palate is vibrating against my posterior pharyngeal wall. (A physiological description of snoring) Apparently, the only thing that will help her is to put her elbow in my ribs.

~

See everything, overlook a lot, correct a little. --Pope John XXIII

~

Oh, the wisdom, the foresight and the hindsight, the right sight and the left sight, the north sight and the south sight, the east sight and the west sight, that appeared in that august assembly.   -John Adams on the US Congress

~

Just because you keep all your lights on doesn't mean you're not in the dark.

~

People who count their chickens before they are hatched act very wisely, because chickens run about so absurdly that it is impossible to count them accurately.

-Oscar Wilde

~

The prisoner stood before the judge to hear his sentence. "The jury finds you guilty, and I sentence you to 99 years in prison without parole. Do you have anything you'd like to say?" The prisoner with head down declared, "Yes, Your Honor, this is certainly going to teach me a lesson."   --Harry David Atwood

~

A word to the wise ain't necessary. It's the stupid ones who need the advice.   -Bill Cosby

~

We have too many men of science and too few men of God. We have grasped the mystery of the atom, and rejected the Sermon on the Mount. The world has achieved brilliance without wisdom, power without conscience. Ours is a world of nuclear giants and ethical infants. We know more about war than we know about peace, more about killing than we do about living.   —US General Omar Bradley

~

An Englishman will burn his bed to catch a flea. -Turkish Proverb

~

The science teacher asked the children what is more important: the sun or the moon. After a long discussion they offered this conclusion. "The moon is more important because it shines at night when you really need the light. The sun only shines in the daytime when there is enough light already."

~

IF IT AIN'T BROKE, DON'T FIX IT.

~

Who is wise? He that learns from everyone.
Who is powerful? He that governs his passions.
Who is rich? He that is content.
Who is that? . . . Nobody.
--Benjamin Franklin

~

It's easier to be wise for others than for ourselves. -La Rochefoucauld

~

The leader of the Altadena Search and Rescue Team, Greg Gabriel, said after rescuing two dozen Cal Tech students who were stuck on Mount Wilson wearing tutus, Superman Capes, and other strange attire, "You've got to remember that common sense is not factored into the intelligent quotient."

-"Newsweek Magazine" 2/13/06

~

WORRY

Bishop William A. Quayle went to bed one night, but sleep escaped him. He was distracted by problems he couldn't solve. Then he heard God speak: "Quayle, go to sleep. I'll sit up the rest of the night." -Charles Wallis, *A Treasury of Sermon Illustrations*

~

When Mark Twain was asked why he didn't read health books. He replied, "One could die of a misprint."

~

I have never yet met a healthy person who worries very much about his health, or a really good person who worries much about his own soul.
- J.B.S. Haldane, 1892-1964

~

An old humor magazine, brown with age, called worry, "the disease of the age." It went on to say that worry is the inevitable result of our mad attempt to run everything, including our own insides, with our minds.

~

It's a troublesome world, all the people in it
Are troubled with troubles almost every minute.
You ought to be thankful, a whole heaping lot,
For the places and people you're lucky you're not.
-Dr. Seuss

~

If you want to test your memory, try to remember what you were worrying about one year ago today.
-E. Joseph Cossman

~

When men wore nightshirts, somebody asked an old fellow if he slept with his beard inside or outside of his nightshirt. He didn't seem to know. But he said, "I'll find out tonight." So he tried it inside and that didn't seem to be right; so he tried it outside, but that didn't seem right either. He died of exhaustion, they say, rearranging his beard.

-Unknown

~

I love to watch football and particularly the play of the linebackers. A linebacker does his job well when he is oblivious to the threats around him. He follows his assignment and goes to the ball carrier with a sense of abandon. But the moment he begins to wonder which one of those 300-pound behemoths is coming after him, two things are going to happen: one, he will not do his job; and two, in the language of the trade, he is going to get creamed.

~

The reason why worry kills more people than work is that more people worry than work.

−Robert Frost

~

When I find myself worrying and analyzing every single detail of my life, I gain some perspective remembering that great line from Thorton Wilder's Play, "The Skin of Our Teeth." "My advice to you is not to inquire why or whither, but just enjoy the ice cream while it's on your plate."

~

A day of worry is more exhausting than a week of work. –Anonymous

~

WHY WORRY?
There are only two things to worry about.
Either you are well or you are sick.
If you are well there's nothing to worry about.
If you are sick there are two things to worry about.
Either you will get well or you will die.
If you get well there is nothing to worry about.
If you die there are only two things to worry about.
Either you will go to heaven or hell.
If you go to heaven there is nothing to worry about.
But if you go to hell, you'll be so busy shaking hands
With your friends, you won't have time to worry.
-Estelle Romero

~

Worry is the interest we pay on tomorrow's troubles. –E. Stanley Jones

~

Don't tell me that worry doesn't do any good. I know better. The things I worry about don't happen.

–Anonymous

~

Worry gives a small thing a big shadow. –Swedish Proverb

~

The Leaven of Laughter Series

WONDER WHAT'S AROUND
THE BEND

The Leaven of Laughter
  For Lent and Easter
The Leaven of Laughter
  About Being Human
The Leaven of Laughter
  It's All About Money
The Leaven of Laughter
  The Bible and Theology
The Leaven of Laughter
  From Arguments to Nuclear War
The Leaven of Laughter
  The Fruits of the Spirit and Other Virtues
The Leaven of Laughter
  The Works of the Flesh and Other Sins
The Leaven of Laughter
  The Work and Worship of the Church
The Leaven of Laughter
  Organized Religion (The Church as Organization)